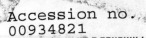

SKETCHES AND TRAVELS
IN LONDON

W.M. THACKERAY

SKETCHES AND TRAVELS
IN LONDON

ALAN SUTTON

ALAN SUTTON PUBLISHING
BRUNSWICK ROAD · GLOUCESTER

First published as a series of articles 1844–50
First published as *Travels in London* 1853

British Library Cataloguing in Publication Data

Thackeray, W.M. (William Makepeace), (1811–1863)
    Sketches and travels in London
    I. Title
    828'.807

    ISBN 0-86299-637-6

Cover picture: detail from Forfeits *by Eyre Crowe.*
Fine Art Photographics Library.

Typesetting and origination
by Alan Sutton Publishing Limited.
Photoset Bembo 9/10
Printed in Great Britain
by The Guernsey Press Company Limited,
Guernsey, Channel Islands.

CONTENTS

BIOGRAPHICAL NOTE

WILLIAM MAKEPEACE THACKERAY (1811–63). A photograph of Thackeray taken a few years before his death at fifty-two shows him to be a well-dressed hefty man (he was six foot three inches, and fifteen stone in his forties), with white hair, clean-shaven, with a well-defined mouth, broad-nosed and bespectacled. Behind the spectacles, even in a photograph, the sparkle and depth of his eyes show humour, sadness and insight.

Although Thackeray achieved his ambition of becoming a famous writer, his personal life was one of almost unremitting sadness, relieved only by his loving relationship with his two daughters. His personal experiences and the characters he knew were to be the substance of most of his fictional writing.

He was born in Calcutta, India, on 18 July 1811, the only child of Anne and Richmond Thackeray. The Thackeray family were a well-established Yorkshire family, with branches at Cambridge, as well as in India. When William was four, his father died, and his mother married a previous lover, Captain Henry Carmichael-Smyth. Thackeray, meanwhile, was sent to England, to be looked after by his paternal aunt and his maternal grandmother. He went to school at Chiswick Mall, with a disastrous interlude at an inhumane school in Southampton, until his adored mother and respected step-father returned from India in 1820. Then he transferred to Charterhouse, one of the better public schools, but Thackeray was no scholar, and although he was intelligent and ambitious, with a love of reading and the theatre, he showed little persistence in his studies.

This lack of application continued when, after a long break in Devon at his parents' home, he finally went up to Trinity College, Cambridge. He stayed there for only sixteen months, his good intentions to study being continually shattered by his attraction to lascivious indulgences, including the gambling table, and his unfortunate liaisons with disreputable characters. However, he made his literary debut in *The Snob* and continued writing for it and its successor, *The Gownsman*, as well as meeting literary men who were to be his friends and acquaintances in the future, among them: Edward Fitzgerald, Tennyson, and William Brookfield. For the next few years, after leaving Cambridge, he lived extravagantly: he spent some months in Weimar, where he met Goethe, fell in love, gambled and learnt German. He then returned to London, and after spending a year deciding not to study law, and then running a literary newspaper at a loss, he retreated to Paris to study art as a poverty-stricken student (since his father's fortune had been mismanaged). Here he met and fell in love with Isabella Shawe. He resolved to marry her in spite of her mother's disapproval, and was pleased to accept the post of French correspondent for *The Constitutional*, a radical newspaper launched with financial assistance from his stepfather. He also produced his first book: *Flore et Zéphyr*, a satire, in 1836, and continued to endeavour to establish himself as an artist.

By July 1837 Thackeray was married to Isabella, a father to baby Annie and unemployed, as *The Constitutional* had folded, and so he was forced to become a freelance journalist, to escape debtor's prison (a situation he explores in *Samuel Titmarsh and the Great Hoggarty Diamond*). He worked as a book reviewer, art critic, poet and serial writer for *The Times*, *Fraser's Magazine*, Dicken's journal *Bentley's Miscellany* and the *New Monthly Magazine*. In 1839 the Thackerays' second daughter died shortly after her birth (another experience relived in *The Great Hoggarty Diamond*), but one year later another girl, Minnie, was born, and Thackeray saw the successful publication of *The Paris Sketch Book*, which received good reviews and interested the important publishing houses of Chapman and Hall, and Longmans. So Thackeray was now an established writer, able to support, if modestly, his young family. However, a happy family life was not to be his, since very soon after the birth of Minnie, Isabella showed the first signs of madness which was to change her personality, and force Thackeray finally to realise that she would never be cured, and to accept a permanent separation. During these unhappy years he wrote *The History of Samuel Titmarsh and the Great Hoggarty Diamond* (first published in *Bentley's Miscellany*) and then made his first claim to fame as a full length novelist with *Barry Lyndon* (1844). However, the latter was unfavourably received as morally outrageous. In the meantime, he had started to write for *Punch*, and in 1846 he made his first significant impact on Victorian society with his study of English society in *The Snobs of England*. This was followed in 1847 by the first episode of *Vanity Fair*, which was to put Thackeray into the same literary class as the great Dickens, then publishing *Dombey and Son*, and to reintroduce him to the aristocratic circles of London society.

Thackeray had installed his family in a house in Young Street, and was comforted by the memory of the early days of his marriage, his present fame and the company of his daughters. But his heart was lonely for the love of a woman. Consequently he was unable to resist a developing passion for Jane, the young and attractive wife of his old Cambridge friend, William Brookfield. She was Thackeray's 'perfect woman'. He loved her whole-heartedly, and it is this love which pervades *Pendennis*, an autobiographical novel, written 1848–50. But the relationship was doomed since the Brookfields were determined to stay together in spite of their incompatability and finally Thackeray was compelled to break away from both William and Jane. In *The History of Henry Esmond*, completed in 1852 after his separation from the Brookfields, he further explores the comotions of an unhappy marriage, like that of the Brookfields, the frustrated lover and the dominant mother figure. (As an only child, Thackeray was adored and to some extent dominated by his possessive strong-willed mother throughout his whole life.) *Henry Esmond*, set in the early eighteenth century, was his most carefully prepared work: 'Here is the very best I can do . . .', and did not suffer from the fact that Thackeray was seldom at home when he wrote. He had decided, after the publication of *Pendennis* to find another more reliable source of income than writing and had taken up lecturing, a comparatively easy way of making money, and positively lucrative when taken across the Atlantic.

After successful tours in England, he lectured in the States for six months, returning in May 1853, having once again fallen in love, and once again futilely. He knew that Sally Baxter was too young for him. Nevertheless, he was upset by her marriage two years later, and kept in touch with her until her lonely death from tuberculosis in 1862. Sally provided the inspiration for Ethel, the heroine of Thackeray's next novel, *The Newcomes* (1853–5), which again tackled problems of marriage and mothers, and was to be set partly in Rome. To this end, Thackeray took his two daughters to Italy, where he contracted malaria, which was to trouble him for the rest of his life, along with occasional outbreaks of a longstanding and painful bowel condition. It was during the illness in Italy that Thackeray wrote *The Rose and the Ring*, with the close collaboration of a little girl called Edith Story.

When the Thackerays returned to England in 1854 it was to a new house in Onslow Square, with Amy Crowe as companion to Annie and Minnie. Very soon Thackeray was planning a return visit to the States, to lay by some capital for his daughters by giving another lecture tour, this time on the four English King Georges. The expedition was financially successful, but Thackeray was upset by some negative press criticism. However, he came home to deliver the same lectures in England and Scotland. In 1857, with the offer of £6000 for a new serial outstanding, and his name made both as novelist and lecturer, Thackeray made his only stand for Parliament, for the City of Oxford, and was defeated by sixty-five votes. Unsurprised by the result, Thackeray returned to London to concentrate on his next novel, *The Virginians* (1859), which contained English and American characters, and was well received in England and the States.

Thackeray, by now a wealthy man, was able, at the age of forty-nine to achieve his last ambition: to edit his own literary paper. This was the *Cornhill Magazine*, which first appeared in 1860. Contributions included George Eliot, Anthony Trollope, Tennyson and Thackeray himself. He published *The Roundabout Papers*, a notable collection of essays, and his final completed novel: *The Adventures of Philip on his Way Through the World*. His final extravagant gesture was to rebuild a house, No. 2, Palace Green, Kensington, where he lived for only two years in increasingly poor health, until his death in 1863 from a brain haemorrhage. He was buried in Kensal Green.

SHEILA MICHELL

INTRODUCTION

This collection of articles describes London life in the 1840s in a similar way to the more famous *Book of Snobs*, but has a strength and interest of its own. Although there are frequent examples of Thackeray's wit and his powers of observation, there is also a sternness and a directness in his criticism of Victorian society that are made all the more effective by contrasting with the preceding humour – though even in his darkest passages he cannot resist a light-hearted sally against his contemporary and rival, Dickens.

The Sketches are parly in the form of letters from the fictional Mr Brown to his nephew, Robert, and are a mixture of criticism of Victorian London and practical advice on how to succeed in it; advice spiced with the casual cynicism that is Thackeray's hallmark.

Thackeray pursues the relationships between the sexes as a prime subject for discussion in many of the articles, and the various stages associated with them. In his own class, courtship was frequently conducted at balls during the London season, so he offers advice about their organization, describing how he tactfully tried to dissuade a heavily-built mother from insisting on accompanying her daughter to a modest sized house which would already be overpopulated with chaperones:

> 'And pray who told you, Mr Brown, that I didn't wish to dance myself?' says Blanche, surveying her great person in the looking-glass (which could scarce contain it) and flouncing out of the room; and I actually believe that the unconscionable creature, at her age and size, is still thinking that she is a fairy, and that the young fellows would like to dance round the room with her.

Marriage was the desired end of the hectic social whirl in the fashionable parts of the capital, and Mr Brown has several

anecdotes to use in warning his nephew against an injudicious
marriage, by which he means an alliance with a girl of a class
much above or below his own, prefacing them with the
remark that:

> Of course you will take my advice, my dear Bob, about
> your flame. All men and women do. It is notorious that
> they listen to the opinions of all their friends, and never
> follow their own counsel.

Speaking of women in general, he remarks that his admiration for them grows with every year, and that their seeming
submissiveness and frivolity is the front for an artful person
skilled at coping with the vanity of a husband:

> You see a demure-looking woman perfect in all her
> duties, constant in house-bills and shirt-buttons . . .
> Benighted idiot! She has long ago taken your measure and
> your friends'; she knows your weaknesses and ministers
> to them in a thousand artful ways. She knows your
> obstinate points, and marches round them with the most
> curious art and patience, as you will see an ant on a
> journey turn round an obstacle . . .

My Brown's own marriage is referred to with less than total
romanticism:

> An exquisite slave is what we want for the most part . . .
> who laughs at our jokes, however old they may be, and
> fondly lies to us through life. I never could get your Aunt
> into this system, though I confess I should have been a
> happier man had she tried it. . . . Poor dear Mrs Brown
> was a far finer woman than Emily Blenkinsop, and yet I
> loved Emily's little finger more than the whole hand
> which your Aunt Martha gave me. . . .

The children are also discussed with a refreshing lack of the
sentimentality that so characterized Victorian attitudes to
children. Thackeray candidly describes the reality of children's
parties:

An odious, revolting and disagreeable practice, sir. . . .
The real satirist has no right to describe a child's ball as if
it was a sort of paradise . . . the little imps . . . happy and
pretty as so many cherubs. They should be drawn, one
and all, as hideous – distorted – affected – jealous of each
other – dancing awkwardly . . . over-eating themselves
at supper – very unwell (and deservedly so) the next
morning . . .

Although in reality a married man who was immensely
fond of his daughters, Thackeray describes, in 'On the
Pleasures of Being a Fogy', some advantages that the onset of
middle age can bring to a bachelor, who may enjoy the
company and conversation of women friends rather than
mooning over a single object of affection. Although that stage
of life has its benefits, Fogies need to remember their obliga-
tions to the younger generation:

When the people are marching out to dinner . . . and the
Captain is sidling up to Miss . . . I become interested in a
picture, or have something particular to say to Polly the
parrot, or to little Tommy . . . and while I am talking to
him, Miss and the Captain make their little arrangement.

In 'Mr Brown the Elder takes Mr Brown the Younger to a
Club', Thackeray describes a visit to the Reform Club, easily
identifiable by the references to its huge and many mirrors:

Sardanapalus, if he had pawned one of his kingdoms,
could not have had such mirrors as one of those in which I
see my dear Bob admiring the tie of his cravat with such
complacency . . .

Having passed the club servants guarding the entrance:

a fifteen-hundredth part of each of whom is henceforth
your paid-for property – and you know as he takes down
your name as Mr R. Brown, Junior, and will know you
and be civil to you unto death . . .

the pair make their way to the library, which is pleasantly empty:

> There is never anybody here. English gentlemen get up such a prodigious quantity of knowledge in their early life, that they leave off reading soon after they begin to shave . . .

A far more serious note is struck into two of the later chapters. In 'Waiting at the Station', he describes emigrant women off to start a new life in Australia, where they will be free from the humiliations of the English class system:

> Let us get her last curtsey from her as she stands here upon the English shore. When she gets into the Australian woods her back won't bend except to her labour . . . do you suppose her children will be like that timid creature you see before you? They will know nothing of this Gothic society, with its ranks and heirarchies, its cumbrous ceremonies . . .

This chapter is extraordinarily powerful, a completely serious attack on the snobberies and obeisance to rank whose various manifestations are so humorously pilloried in the *Book of Snobs* and other articles in the *Sketches and Travels in London*. Thackeray, however, was far from being a socialist, being very aware of his upper middle class status and the social distance that this background placed between, for example, his fellow writers for *Punch* and himself.

Earlier in this book, for example, he advised his fictional nephew that:

> It may safely be asserted that the persons who joke with servants or barmaids . . . are not men of high intellectual or moral capacity . . . the youthful grocer may exchange a few jocular remarks with Betty at the door . . . but not you. We must live according to our degree.

Yet in 'Waiting at the Station' he flays this very attitude, that the two classes almost belong to different species, that any real relations between them other than that of servant and master is too ridiculous to contemplate, other than as a joke. This article, which could almost serve as a sermon, is not a political statement, but a moral one. Thackeray was not calling for a revolution, but for people to behave with a basic respect for others. In 'Going to See a Man Hanged' he describes his horror at seeing another human being done to death, and the brutalizing effect on the huge crowd of onlookers, who regarded the spectacle as entertainment. He accuses the lower classes of the same lack of imagination and decency as their social superiors. Even here, however, he cannot resist an aside, criticizing writers and artists for glamourizing their subjects to make them more acceptable to the middle classes – as with Bill Sykes' mistress:

> There were a considerable number of girls . . . one that . . . Boz might have taken as a study for Nancy. . . . Both of these women had beautiful eyes, an admirably fair complexion, and a large red mouth full of white teeth. *Au reste*, ugly, stunted, thick-limbed . . .

Even at such a dreadful spectacle he cannot resist observing individuals, their looks and mannerisms, their character and how other writers have portrayed similar types. It is this interest in his fellow creatures, as much as his pity for the criminal who died as an object of amusement and recreation, that demonstrates Thackeray's humanity, and which gave him such an eye for the weaknesses of others and of the society in which he lived.

This humanity and his skill in expressing it dominates this book, whose chapters blend his flippant cynicism and worldly humour with chivalry, affection, and a morality that raises some of his writing up to and beyond the levels reached in Dickens' better-known outbursts against injustice. In reading this book, we can understand Thackeray's success as a humourist, his reputation as a skillful journalist and commentator on human nature, and the moral force, combined with clubbable good nature, that made his early death, aged fifty-two, such a blow. As the *Dictionary of National Biography* recorded, 'few deaths were received with more general expressions of sorrow.'

PAUL I. WEBB

SKETCHES AND TRAVELS
IN LONDON

SKETCHES
AND
TRAVELS IN LONDON

MR BROWN'S LETTERS TO HIS NEPHEW

t is with the greatest satisfaction, my dear Robert, that I have you as a neighbour, within a couple of miles of me, and that I have seen you established comfortably in your chambers in Fig-tree Court. The situation is not cheerful, it is true; and to clamber up three pairs of black creaking stairs is an exercise not pleasant to a man who never cared for ascending mountains. Nor did the performance of the young barrister who lives under you – and, it appears, plays pretty constantly upon the French horn – give me any great pleasure as I sat and partook of luncheon in your rooms. Your female attendant or laundress, too, struck me from her personal appearance to be a lady addicted to the use of ardent spirits; and the smell of tobacco, which you say some old college friends of yours had partaken on the night previous, was, I must say, not pleasant in the chambers, and I even thought might be remarked as lingering in your own morning-coat. However, I am an old fellow. The use of cigars has come in since my time (and, I must own, is adopted by many people of the first fashion), and these and other inconveniences are surmounted more gaily by

1

young fellows like yourself than by oldsters of my standing. It pleased me, however, to see the picture of the old house at home over the mantelpiece. Your college prize-books make a very good show in your bookcases; and I was glad to remark in the looking-glass the cards of both our excellent county Members. The rooms, altogether, have a reputable appearance; and I hope, my dear fellow, that the Society of the Inner Temple will have a punctual tenant.

As you have now completed your academical studies, and are about to commence your career in London, I propose, my dear Nephew, to give you a few hints for your guidance; which, although you have an undoubted genius of your own, yet come from a person who has had considerable personal experience, and, I have no doubt, would be useful to you if you did not disregard them, as, indeed, you will most probably do.

With your law studies it is not my duty to meddle. I have seen you established, one of six pupils, in Mr Tapeworm's chambers in Pump Court, seated on a high-legged stool on a foggy day, with your back to a blazing fire. At your father's desire, I have paid a hundred guineas to that eminent special pleader, for the advantages which I have no doubt you will enjoy, while seated on the high-legged stool in his back room, and rest contented with your mother's prediction that you will be Lord Chief Justice some day. May you prosper, my dear fellow is all I desire. By the way, I should like to know what was the meaning of a pot of porter which entered into your chambers as I issued from them at one o'clock, and trust that it was not *your* thirst which was to be quenched with such a beverage at such an hour.

It is not, then, with regard to your duties as a law-student that I have a desire to lecture you, but in respect of your pleasures, amusements, acquaintances, and general conduct and bearing as a young man of the world.

I will rush into the subject at once, and exemplify my morality in your own person. Why, sir, for instance, do you wear that tuft to your chin, and those sham turquoise buttons to your waistcoat? A chin-tuft is a cheap enjoyment certainly, and the twiddling it about, as I see you do constantly, so as to show your lower teeth, a harmless amusement to fill up your vacuous hours. And as for waistcoat buttons, you will say, 'Do not all the young men wear them, and what can I do but buy artificial turquoise, as I cannot afford to buy real stones?'

I take you up at once and show you why you ought to shave off your tip and give up the factitious jewellery. My dear Bob, in spite of us and all the Republicans in the world, there are ranks and degrees in life and society, and distinctions to be maintained by each man according to his rank and degree. You have no more right, as I take it, to sport an imperial on your chin than I have to wear a shovel-hat with a rosette. I hold a tuft to a man's chin to be the centre of a system, so to speak, which ought all to correspond and be harmonious – the whole tune of a man's life ought to be played in that key.

Look, for instance, at Lord Hugo Fitzurse seated in the private box at the Lyceum, by the side of that beautiful creature with the black eyes and the magnificent point-lace, who you fancied was ogling you through her enormous spy-glasses. Lord Hugo has a tuft to his chin, certainly, his countenance grins with a perfect vacuity behind it, and his whiskers curl crisply round one of the handsomest and stupidest countenances in the world.

But just reckon up in your own mind what it costs him to keep up that simple ornament on his chin. Look at every article of that amiable and most gentleman-like – though, I own, foolish – young man's dress, and see how absurd it is of you to attempt to imitate him. Look at his hands (I have the young nobleman perfectly before my mind's eye now); the little hands are dangling over the cushion of the box gloved as tightly and delicately as a lady's. His wristbands are fastened up towards his elbows with jewellery. Gems and rubies meander down his pink shirt-front and waistcoat. He wears a watch with an apparatus of gimcracks at his waistcoat-pocket. He sits in a splendid side-box, or he simpers out of the windows at 'White's', or you see him grinning out of a cab by the Serpentine – a lovely and costly picture, surrounded by a costly frame.

Whereas you and I, my good Bob, if we want to see a play, do not disdain an order from our friend the newspaper Editor, or to take a seat in the pit. Your watch is your father's old hunting-watch. When we go in the Park we go on foot, or at

best get a horse up after Easter, and just show in Rotten Row.
We shall never look out of 'White's' bow-window. The
amount of Lord Hugo's tailor's bill would support you and
your younger brother. His valet has as good an allowance as
you, besides, his perquisites of old clothes. You cannot afford
to wear a dandy lord's cast-off old clothes, neither to imitate
those which he wears.

There is nothing disagreeable to me in the notion of a dandy
any more than there is in the idea of a peacock, or a
camelopard, or a prodigious gaudy tulip, or an astonishingly
bright brocade. There are all sorts of animals, plants, and
stuffs in Nature, from peacocks to tom-tits, and from cloth of
gold to corduroy, whereof the variety is assuredly intended by
Nature, and certainly adds to the zest of life. Therefore, I do
not say that Lord Hugo is a useless being, or bestow the least
contempt upon him. Nay, it is right gratifying and natural
that he should be, and be as he is – handsome and graceful,
splendid and perfumed, beautiful – whiskered and empty-
headed, a sumptuous dandy and man of fashion – and what
you young men have denominated 'A Swell'.

But a cheap Swell, my dear Robert (and that little chin
ornament, as well as certain other indications which I have
remarked in your simple nature, lead me to insist upon this
matter rather strongly with you), is by no means a pleasing
object for our observation, although he is presented to us so
frequently. Try, my boy, and curb any little propensity which
you may have to dresses that are too splendid for your station.
You do not want light kid-gloves and wristbands up to your
elbows, copying out Mr Tapeworm's Pleas and Declarations;
you will only blot them with lawyer's ink over your desk, and
they will impede your writing: whereas Lord Hugo may
decorate his hands in any way he likes, because he has little else
to do with them but to drive cabs, or applaud dancing-girls'
pirouettes, or to handle a knife and fork or a tooth-pick as
becomes the position in life which he fills in so distinguished a
manner. To be sure, since the days of friend Aesop, Jackdaws
have been held up to ridicule for wearing the plumes of birds
to whom Nature has affixed more gaudy tails; but as Folly is
constantly reproducing itself, so must Satire, and our honest
Mr Punch has but to repeat to the men of our generation the

lessons taught by the good-natured Hunchback his pre-decessor.

Shave off your tuft, then, my boy, and send it to the girl of your heart as a token, if you like: and I pray you abolish the jewellery, towards which I clearly see you have a propensity. As you have a plain dinner at home, served comfortably on a clean tablecloth, and not a grand service of half a dozen *entrées*, such as we get at our county Member's (and an uncommonly good dinner it is too), so let your dress be perfectly neat, polite, and cleanly, without any attempts at splendour. Magnificence is the decency of the rich – but it cannot be purchased with half a guinea a day, which, when the rent of your chambers is paid, I take to be pretty nearly the amount of your worship's income. This point, I thought, was rather well illustrated the other day, in an otherwise silly and sentimental book which I looked over at the Club, called the 'Foggarty Diamond' (or some such vulgar name). Somebody gives the hero, who is a poor fellow, a diamond pin: he is obliged to buy a new stock to set off the diamond, then a new waistcoat, to correspond with the stock, then a new coat, because the old one is too shabby for the rest of his attire; – finally, the poor devil is ruined by the diamond ornament, which he is forced to sell, as I would recommend you to sell your waistcoat studs, were they worth anything.

But as you have a good figure and a gentleman-like deportment, and as every young man likes to be well attired, and ought, for the sake of his own advantage and progress in life, to show himself to the best advantage, I shall take an early opportunity of addressing you on the subject of tailors and clothes, which at least merit a letter to themselves.

ON TAILORING – AND TOILETTES IN GENERAL

ur ancestors, my dear Bob, have transmitted to you (as well as every member of our family), considerable charms of person and figure, of which fact, although you are of course perfectly aware, yet, and equally of course, you have no objection to be reminded; and with these facial and corporeal endowments, a few words respecting dress and tailoring may not be out of place; for nothing is trivial in life, and everything to the philosopher has a meaning. As in the old joke about a pudding which has two sides, namely an inside and an outside, so a coat or a hat has its inside as well as its outside; I mean, that there is in a man's exterior appearance the consequence of his inward ways of thought, and a gentleman who dresses too grandly, or too absurdly, or too shabbily, has some oddity, or insanity, or meanness in his mind, which develops itself somehow outwardly in the fashion of his garments.

No man has a right to despise his dress in this world. There is no use in flinging any honest chance whatever away. For instance, although a woman cannot be expected to know the particulars of a gentleman's dress, any more than we to be acquainted with the precise nomenclature or proper cut of the various articles which those dear creatures wear, yet to what lady in a society of strangers do we feel ourselves most naturally inclined to address ourselves? – to her or those whose appearance pleases us; not to the gaudy, overdressed Dowager or Miss – nor to her whose clothes, though handsome, are put on in a slatternly manner, but to the person who looks neat, and trim, and elegant, and in whose person we fancy we see exhibited indications of a natural taste, order, and propriety. If Miss Smith in a rumpled gown offends our eyesight, though we hear she is a young lady of great genius and considerable fortune, while Miss Jones in her trim and simple attire attracts our admiration; so must women, on their side, be attracted or repelled by the appearance of gentlemen into whose company they fall. If you are a tiger in appearance, you may naturally expect to frighten a delicate and timid female; if you are a sloven, to offend her: and as to be well with women, constitutes one of the chiefest happinesses of life, the object of my worthy Bob's special attention will naturally be, to neglect no precautions to win their favour.

Yes: a good face, a good address, a good dress, are each so many points in the game of life, of which every man of sense will avail himself. They help many a man more in his commerce with society than learning or genius. It is hard often to bring the former into a drawing-room: it is often too lumbering and unwieldy for any den but its own. And as a King Charles's spaniel can snooze before the fire, or frisk over the ottoman-cushions and on to the ladies' laps, when a Royal elephant would find a considerable difficulty in walking up the stairs, and subsequently in finding a seat; so a good manner and appearance will introduce you into many a house, where you might knock in vain for admission, with all the learning of Porson in your trunk.

It is not learning, it is not virtue, about which people inquire in society. It is manners. It no more profits me that my neighbour at table can construe Sanscrit and say the 'Encyclopaedia' by heart, than that he should possess half a million in the Bank (unless, indeed, he gives dinners; when, for reasons obvious, one's estimation of him, or one's desire to please him, takes its rise in different sources), or that the lady whom I hand down to dinner should be as virtuous as Cornelia or the late Mrs Hannah More. What is wanted for the nonce is, that folks should be as agreeable as possible in conversation and demeanour; so that good humour may be said to be one of the very best articles of dress one can wear in society; the which to see exhibited in Lady X's honest face, let us say, is more pleasant to behold in a room than the glitter of Lady Z's best diamonds. And yet, in point of virtue, the latter is, no doubt, a perfect dragon. But virtue is a home quality: manners are the coat it wears when it goes abroad.

Thus, then, my beloved Bob, I would have your dining-out suit handsome, neat, well-made, fitting you naturally and easily, and yet with a certain air of holiday about it, which should mark its destination. It is not because they thought their appearance was much improved by the ornament, that the ancient philosophers and topers decorated their old pates with flowers (no wreath, I know, would make some people's mugs beautiful; and I confess, for my part, I would as lief wear a horse-collar or a cotton nightcap in society as a coronet of polyanthuses or a garland of hyacinths): – it is not because a philosopher cares about dress that he wears it; but he wears his best as a sign of a feast, as a bush is the sign of an inn. You ought to mark a festival as a red letter day, and you put on your broad and spotless white waistcoat, your finest linen, your shiniest boots, as much as to say, 'It is a feast; here I am, clean, smart, ready with a good appetite, determined to enjoy.'

You would not enjoy a feast if you came to it unshorn, in a draggle-tailed dressing-gown. You ought to be well dressed, and suitable to it. A very old and wise man whom I once knew, and who had not (as far as one could outwardly judge) the least vanity about his personal appearance, used, I remember, to make a point of wearing in large Assemblies a most splendid gold or crimson waistcoat. He seemed to consider himself in the light of a walking bouquet of flowers, or a moveable chandelier. His waistcoat was a piece of furniture to decorate the rooms: as for any personal pride he took in the adornment, he had none: for the matter of that, he would have taken the garment off, and lent it to a waiter – but this

Philosopher's maxim was, that dress should be handsome upon handsome occasions – and I hope you will exhibit your own taste upon such. You don't suppose that people who entertain you so hospitably have four-and-twenty lights in the dining-room, and still and dry champagne every day? – or that my friend, Mrs Perkins, puts her drawing-room door under her bed every night, when there is no ball? A young fellow must dress himself, as the host and hostess dress themselves, in an extra manner for extra nights. Enjoy, my boy, in honesty and manliness, the goods of this life. I would no more have you refuse to take your glass of wine, or to admire (always in honesty) a pretty girl, than dislike the smell of a rose, or turn away your eyes from a landscape. '*Neque tu choreas sperne, puer*', as the dear old Heathen says: and, in order to dance, you must have proper pumps willing to spring and whirl lightly, and a clean pair of gloves, with which you can take your partner's pretty little hand.

As for particularising your dress, that were a task quite absurd and impertinent, considering that you are to wear it, and not I, and remembering the variations of fashion. When I was presented to HRH the Prince Regent, in the uniform of the Hammersmith Hussars, viz. a yellow jacket, pink pantaloons, and silver lace, green morocco boots, and a light blue pelisse lined with ermine, the august Prince himself, the model of grace and elegance in his time, wore a coat of which the waist-buttons were placed between his royal shoulder blades, and which, if worn by a man now, would cause the boys to hoot him in Pall Mall, and be a uniform for Bedlam. If buttons continue their present downward progress, a man's waist may fall down to his heels next year, or work upwards to the nape of his neck after another revolution: who knows? Be it yours decently to conform to the custom, and leave your buttons in the hands of a good tailor, who will place them wherever fashion ordains. A few general rules, however, may be gently hinted to a young fellow who has perhaps a propensity to fall into certain errors.

Eschew violent sporting-dresses, such as one sees but too often in the parks and public places on the backs of misguided young men. There is no objection to an ostler wearing a particular costume, but it is a pity that a gentleman should imitate it. I have seen in like manner young fellows at Cowes attired like the pictures we have of smugglers, buccaneers, and mariners in Adelphi melodramas. I would like my Bob to remember, that his business in life is neither to handle a currycomb nor a marlin-spike, and to fashion his habit accordingly.

If your hair or clothes do not smell of tobacco, as they sometimes, it must be confessed, do, you will not be less popular among ladies. And as no man is worth a fig, or can have real benevolence of character, or observe mankind properly, who does not like the society of modest and well-bred women, respect their prejudices in this matter, and if you must smoke, smoke in an old coat, and away from the ladies.

Avoid dressing-gowns; which argue dawdling, an unshorn chin, a lax toilet, and a general lazy and indolent habit at home. Begin your day with a clean conscience in every way. Cleanliness is honesty.* A man who shows but a clean face and hands is a rogue and hypocrite in society, and takes credit for a virtue which he does not possess. And of all the advances towards civilization which our nation has made, and of most of which Mr Macaulay treats so eloquently in his lately published History, as in his lecture to the Glasgow Students the other day, there is none which ought to give a philanthropist more pleasure than to remark the great and increasing demand for bath tubs at the ironmongers': Zinc-Institutions, of which our ancestors had a lamentable ignorance.

And I hope that these institutions will be universal in our country before long, and that every decent man in England will be a Companion of the Most Honourable Order of the Bath.

---

* *Note to the beloved Reader.* – This hint, dear Sir, is of course not intended to apply personally to *you*, who are scrupulously neat in your person; but when you look around you and see how many people neglect the use of that admirable cosmetic, cold water, you will see that a few words in its praise may be spoken with advantage.

THE INFLUENCE OF LOVELY WOMEN UPON SOCIETY

onstantly, my dear Bob, I have told you how refining is the influence of women upon society, and how profound our respect ought to be for them. Living in chambers as you do, my dear Nephew, and not of course liable to be amused by the constant society of an old uncle, who moreover might be deucedly bored with your own conversation – I beseech and implore you to make a point of being intimate with one or two families where you can see kind and well-bred English ladies. I have seen women of all nations in the world, but I never saw the equals of English women (meaning of course to include our cousins the MacWhirters of Glasgow, and the O'Tooles of Cork): and I pray sincerely, my boy, that you may always have a woman for a friend.

Try, then, and make yourself the *bienvenu* in some house where accomplished and amiable ladies are. Pass as much of your time as you can with them. Lose no opportunity of making yourself agreeable to them: run their errands; send them flowers and elegant little tokens; show a willingness to be pleased by their attentions, and to aid their little charming schemes of shopping or dancing, or this, or that. I say to you, make yourself a lady's man as much as ever you can.

It is better for you to pass an evening once or twice a week in a lady's drawing-room, even though the conversation is rather slow and you know the girls' songs by heart, than in a club, tavern, or smoking-room, or a pit of a theatre. All amusements of youth, to which virtuous women are not admitted, are, rely on it, deleterious in their nature. All men who avoid female society, have dull perceptions and are stupid, or have gross tastes and revolt against what is pure. Your Club swaggerers who are sucking the butts of billiard cues all night call female society insipid. Sir, poetry is insipid to a yokel; beauty has no charms for a blind man: music does not please an unfortunate brute who does not know one tune from another – and, as a true epicure is hardly ever tired of water-souchy and brown bread and butter, I protest I can sit for a whole night talking to a well-regulated kindly woman about her girl coming out, or her boy at Eton, and like the evening's entertainment.

One of the great benefits a young man may derive from women's society is, that he is bound to be respectful to them. The habit is of great good to your moral man, depend on it. Our education makes of us the most eminently selfish men in the world. We fight for ourselves, we push for ourselves; we cut the best slices out of the joint at club-dinners for ourselves; we yawn for ourselves and light our pipes, and say we won't go out: we prefer ourselves and our ease – and the greatest good that comes to a man from woman's society is, that he has to think of somebody besides himself – somebody to whom he is bound to be constantly attentive and respectful. Certainly I don't want my dear Bob to associate with those of the other sex whom he doesn't and can't respect: that is worse than billiards: worse than tavern brandy-and-water: worse than smoking selfishness at home. But I vow I would rather see you turning over the leaves of Miss Fiddlecombe's music book all night, than at billiards, or smoking, or brandy-and-water, or all three.

Remember, if a house is pleasant, and you like to remain in it, that to be well with the women of the house is the great, the vital point. If it is a good house, don't turn up your nose because you are only asked to come in the evening while others are invited to dine. Recollect the debts of dinners which a hospitable family has to pay; who are you that you should always be expecting to nestle under the mahogany? Agreeable acquaintances are made just as well in the drawing-room as in the dining-room. Go to tea brisk and good-humoured. Be determined to be pleased. Talk to a Dowager. Take a hand at whist. If you are musical, and know a song, sing it like a man. Never sulk about dancing but off with you. You will find your acquaintance enlarge. Mothers, pleased with your good humour, will probably ask you to Pocklington Square, to a little party. You will get on – you will form yourself a circle. You may marry a rich girl, or, at any rate, get the chance of seeing a number of the kind and the pretty.

Many young men, who are more remarkable for their impudence and selfishness than their good sense, are fond of boastfully announcing that they decline going to evening parties at all, unless, indeed, such entertainments commence with a good dinner, and a quantity of claret.

I never saw my beautiful-minded friend, Mrs YZ, many times out of temper, but can quite pardon her indignation when young Fred Noodle, to whom the YZ's have been very kind, and who has appeared scores of times at their elegant table in Up—r B–k–r Street, announced, in an unlucky moment of flippancy, that he did not intend to go to evening parties any more.

What induced Fred Noodle to utter this bravado I know not; whether it was that he has been puffed up by attentions from several Aldermen's families, with whom he has of late become acquainted, and among whom he gives himself the airs of a prodigious 'swell'; but having made this speech one Sunday after Church, when he condescended to call in B–k–r Street, and show off his new gloves and waistcoat, and talked in a sufficiently dandified air about the opera (the wretched creature fancies that an eight-and-sixpenny pit ticket gives him the privileges of a man of fashion) – Noodle made his bow to the ladies, and strutted off to show his new yellow kids elsewhere.

'Matilda my love, bring the Address Book', Mrs YZ said to her lovely eldest daughter, as soon as Noodle was gone, and the banging hall door had closed upon the absurd youth. That graceful and obedient girl rose, went to the back drawing-room, on a table in which apartment the volume lay, and brought the book to her mamma.

Mrs YZ turned to the letter N; and under that initial discovered the name of the young fellow who had just gone out. Noodle, F., 250, Jermyn Street, St James's. She took a pen from the table before her, and with it deliberately crossed the name of Mr Noodle out of her book. Matilda looked at Eliza, who stood by in silent awe. The sweet eldest girl, who has a kind feeling towards every soul alive, then looked towards her mother with expostulating eyes, and said, 'Oh, mamma!' Dear, dear Eliza! I love all pitiful hearts like thine.

But Mrs YZ was in no mood to be merciful, and gave way to a natural indignation and feeling of outraged justice.

'What business has that young man to tell me,' she exclaimed, 'that he declines going to evening parties, when he knows that after Easter we have one or two? Has he not met with constant hospitality here since Mr YZ brought him home from the Club? Has he such *beaux yeux*? or, has he so much wit? or, is he a man of so much note, that his company at a dinner-table becomes indispensable? He is nobody; he is not handsome; he is not clever; he never opens his mouth except to drink your Papa's claret; and he declines evening parties forsooth! – Mind, children, he is never invited into this house again.'

When YZ now meets young Noodle at the Club, that kind, but feeble-minded old gentleman covers up his face with the newspaper, so as not to be seen by Noodle; or sidles away with his face to the bookcases, and lurks off by the door. The other day, they met on the steps, when the wretched Noodle, driven *aux abois*, actually had the meanness to ask how Mrs YZ was? The Colonel (for such he is, and of the Bombay service, too) said, – 'My wife? Oh! – hum! – I'm sorry to say Mrs YZ has been very poorly indeed, lately, very poorly; and confined to her room. God bless my soul! I've an appointment at the India House, and it's past two o'clock' – and he fled.

I had the malicious satisfaction of describing to Noodle the most sumptuous dinner which YZ had given the day before, at which there was a Lord present, a Foreign Minister with his Orders, two Generals with Stars, and every luxury of the season; but at the end of our conversation, seeing the effect it had upon the poor youth, and how miserably he was cast down, I told him the truth, viz., that the above story was a hoax, and that if he wanted to get into Mrs YZ's good graces again, his best plan was to go to Lady Flack's party, where I knew the Miss Y Z's would be, and dance with them all night.

Yes, my dear Bob, you boys must pay with your persons, however lazy you may be – however much inclined to smoke at the Club, or to lie there and read the last delicious new novel; or averse to going home to a dreadful black set of chambers, where there is no fire; and at ten o'clock at night creeping shuddering into your ball suit, in order to go forth to an evening party.

The dressing, the clean gloves, and cab hire are nuisances, I grant you. The idea of a party itself is a bore, but you must go. When you are at the party, it is not so stupid; there is always something pleasant for the eye and attention of an observant man. There is a bustling Dowager wheedling and manoeuvring to get proper partners for her girls; there is a pretty girl enjoying herself with all her heart, and in all the pride of her beauty, than which I know no more charming object; – there is poor Miss Meggot, lonely up against the wall, whom nobody asks to dance, and with whom it is your bounden duty to waltz. There is always something to see or do, when you are there; and to evening parties, I say, you must go.

Perhaps I speak with the ease of an old fellow who is out of the business, and beholds you from afar off. My dear boy, they don't want *us* at evening parties. A stout, bald-headed man dancing, is a melancholy object to himself in the looking glass opposite, and there are duties and pleasures of all ages. Once, heaven help us, and only once, upon my honour, and I say so as a gentleman, some boys seized upon me and carried me to the Casino, where, forthwith, they found acquaintances and partners, and went whirling away in the double-timed waltz (it is an abominable dance to me – I am an old fogy) along with hundreds more. I caught sight of a face in the crowd – the most blank, melancholy, and dreary old visage it was – my own face in the glass – there was no use in my being there. *Canities adest morosa* – no, not *morosa* – but, in fine, I had no business in the place, and so came away.

I saw enough of that Casino, however, to show to me that – but my paper is full, and on the subject of women I have more things to say, which might fill many hundred more pages.

SOME MORE WORDS ABOUT THE LADIES

Suffer me to continue, my dear Bob, my remarks about women, and their influence over you young fellows – an influence so vast, for good or for evil.

I have, as you pretty well know, an immense sum of money in the Three per Cents. the possession of which does not, I think, decrease your respect for my character, and of which, at my demise, you will possibly have your share. But if I ever hear of you as a Casino haunter, as a frequenter of Races and Greenwich Fairs, and such amusements, in questionable company, I give you my honour you shall benefit from no legacy of mine, and I will divide the portion that was, and is, I hope, to be yours, amongst your sisters.

Think, sir, of what they are, and of your mother at home, spotless and pious, loving and pure, and shape your own course so as to be worthy of them. Would you do anything to give them pain? Would you say anything that should bring a blush to their fair cheeks, or shock their gentle natures? At the Royal Academy Exhibition last year, when that great stupid, dandified donkey, Captain Grigg, in company with the other vulgar oaf, Mr Gowker, ventured to stare, in rather an insolent manner, at your pretty little sister Fanny, who had come blushing from Miss Pinkerton's Academy, I saw how your honest face flushed up with indignation, as you caught a sight of the hideous grins and ogles of those two ruffians in varnished boots; and your eyes flashed out at them glances of defiance and warning so savage and terrible, that the discomfited wretches turned wisely upon their heels, and did not care to face such a resolute young champion as Bob Brown. What is it that makes all your blood tingle, and fills all your heart

16

with a vague and fierce desire to thrash somebody, when the idea of the possibility of an insult to that fair creature enters your mind? You can't bear to think that injury should be done to a being so sacred, so innocent, and so defenceless. You would do battle with a Goliath in her cause. Your sword would leap from its scabbard (that is, if you gentlemen from Pump Court wore swords and scabbards at the present period of time), to avenge or defend her.

Respect all beauty, all innocence, my dear Bob; defend all defencelessness in your sister, as in the sisters of other men. We have all heard the story of the Gentleman of the last century, who, when a crowd of young bucks and bloods in the Crush-room of the Opera were laughing and elbowing an old lady there – an old lady, lonely, ugly, and unprotected – went up to her respectfully and offered her his arm, took her down to his own carriage which was in waiting, and walked home himself in the rain, – and twenty years afterwards had ten thousand a year left him by this very old lady, as a reward for that one act of politeness. We have all heard that story; nor do I think it is probable that you will have ten thousand a year left to you for being polite to a woman: but I say, be polite, at any rate. Be respectful to every woman. A manly and generous heart can not be otherwise; as a man would be gentle with a child, or take off his hat in a church.

I would have you apply this principle universally towards women – from the finest lady of your acquaintance down to the laundress who sets your Chambers in order. It may safely be asserted that the persons who joke with servants or barmaids at lodgings are not men of a high intellectual or moral capacity. To chuck a still-room maid under the chin, or to send off Molly the cook grinning, are not, to say the least of them, dignified acts in any gentleman. The butcher boy who brings the leg of mutton to Molly, may converse with her over the area railings; or the youthful grocer may exchange a few jocular remarks with Betty at the door as he hands in to her the tea and sugar: but not you. We must live according to our degree. I hint this to you, sir, by the way, and because the other night, as I was standing on the drawing-room landing place, taking leave of our friends Mr and Mrs Fairfax, after a very agreeable dinner, I heard a giggling in the hall, where you were putting on your coat, and where that uncommonly good-looking parlour-maid was opening the door. And here, whilst on this subject, and whilst Mrs Betty is helping you on with your coat, I would say, respecting your commerce with friends' servants and your own, be thankful to them, and they will be grateful to you in return, depend upon it. Let the young fellow who lives in lodgings respect the poor little maid who does the wondrous work of the house, and not send her on too many errands, or ply his bell needlessly: if you visit any of your comrades in such circumstances, be you, too, respectful and kind in your tone to the poor little Abigail. If you frequent houses, as I hope you will, where are many good fellows and amiable ladies who cannot afford to have their doors opened or their tables attended by men, pray be particularly courteous (though by no means so marked in your attentions as on the occasion of the dinner at Mr Fairfax's to which I have just alluded) to the women servants. Thank them when they serve you. Give them a half-crown now and then – nay, as often as your means will permit. Those small gratuities make but a small sum in your year's expenses, and it may be said that the practice of giving them never impoverished a man yet: and, on the other hand, they give a deal of innocent happiness to a very worthy, active, kind set of folks.

But let us hasten from the hall door to the drawing-room, where Fortune has cast your lot in life: I want to explain to you why I am so anxious that you should devote yourself to that amiable lady who sits in it. Sir, I do not mean to tell you that there are no women in the world vulgar and ill-humoured, rancorous and narrow-minded, mean schemers, son-in-law hunters, slaves of fashion, hypocrites; but I do respect, admire, and almost worship good women; and I think there is a very fair number of such to be found in this world, and I have no doubt, in every educated Englishman's circle of society, whether he finds that circle in palaces in Belgravia and Mayfair, in snug little suburban villas, in ancient comfortable old Bloomsbury, or in back parlours behind the shop. It has been my fortune to meet with excellent English ladies in every one of these places – wives graceful and affectionate, matrons tender and good, daughters happy and pure-minded, and I urge the society of such on you, because I defy you to think evil in their company. Walk into the drawing-room of Lady Z, that great lady: look at her charming face, and hear her voice. You know that she can't but be good, with such a face and such a voice. She is one of those fortunate beings on whom it has pleased heaven to bestow all sorts of its most precious gifts and richest worldly favours. With what grace she receives you; with what a frank kindness and natural sweetness and dignity! Her looks, her motions, her words, her thoughts, all seem to be beautiful and harmonious quite. See her with her children, what woman can be more simple and loving? After you have talked to her for a while, you very likely find that she is ten times as well read as you are: she has a hundred accomplishments which she is not in the least anxious to show off, and makes no more account of them than of her diamonds, or of the splendour round about her – to all of which she is born, and has a happy, admirable claim of nature and possession – admirable and happy for her and for us too; for is it not a happiness for us to admire her? Does anybody grudge her excellence to that paragon? Sir, we may be thankful to be admitted to contemplate such consummate goodness and beauty: and as in looking at a fine landscape or a fine work of art, every generous heart must be delighted and improved, and ought to feel grateful afterwards, so one may feel charmed and thankful for having the opportunity of known an almost perfect woman. Madam, if the gout and the custom of the world permitted, I would kneel down and kiss the hem of your ladyship's robe. To see your gracious face is a comfort – to see you walk to your carriage is a holiday. Drive her faithfully, O thou silver-wigged coachman! drive to all sorts of splendours and honours and royal festivals. And for us, let us be glad that we should have the privilege to admire her.

Now, transport yourself in spirit, my good Bob, into another drawing-room. There sits an old lady of more than fourscore years, serene and kind, and as beautiful in her age now as in her youth, when History toasted her. What has she not seen, and what is she not ready to tell? All the fame and wit, all the rank and beauty, of more than half a century, have passed through those rooms where you have the honour of making your best bow. She is as simple now as if she had never had any flattery to dazzle her: she is never tired of being pleased and being kind. Can that have been anything but a good life which, after more than eighty years of it are spent, is so calm? Could she look to the end of it so cheerfully, if its long course had not been pure? Respect her, I say, for being so happy, now that she is old. We do not know what goodness and charity, what affections, what trials, may have gone to make that charming sweetness of temper, and complete that perfect manner. But if we do not admire and reverence such an old age as that, and get good from contemplating it, what are we to respect and admire?

Or shall we walk through the shop (while N is recommending a tall copy to an amateur, or folding up a twopenny-worth of letter paper, and bowing to a poor customer in a jacket and apron with just as much respectful gravity as he would show while waiting upon a Duke), and see Mrs N playing with the child in the back parlour until N shall come into tea? They drink tea at five o'clock; and are actually as well bred as those gentlefolk who dine three hours later. Or will you please to step into Mrs J's lodgings, who is waiting, and at work, until her husband comes home from Chambers? She blushes and puts the work away on hearing the knock, but when she sees who the visitor is, she takes it with a smile from behind the sofa cushion, and behold, it is one of J's waistcoats, on which she is sewing buttons. She might have been a Countess blazing in diamonds, had Fate so willed it, and the higher her station the more she would have adorned it. But she looks as charming while plying her needle as the great lady in the palace whose equal she is, – in beauty, in goodness, in high-bred grace and simplicity: at least, I can't fancy her better, or any Peeress being more than her peer.

And it is with this sort of people, my dear Bob, that I recommend you to consort, if you can be so lucky as to meet with their society – nor do I think you are very likely to find many such at the Casino; or in the dancing booths of Greenwich Fair on this present Easter Monday.

ON FRIENDSHIP

hoice of friends, my dear Robert, is a point upon which every man about town should be instructed, as he should be careful. And as example, they say, is sometimes better than precept, and at the risk even of appearing somewhat ludicrous in your eyes, I will narrate to you an adventure which happened to myself, which is at once ridiculous and melancholy (at least to me), and which will show you how a man, not imprudent or incautious of his own nature, may be made to suffer by the imprudent selection of a friend. Attend then, my dear Bob, to 'the History of Rasselas, Prince of Abyssinia'.

Sir, in the year 1810, I was a jolly young Bachelor, as you are now (indeed, it was three years before I married your poor dear Aunt); I had a place in the Tape and Sealing-Wax Office; I had Chambers in Pump Court, *au troisième*, and led a not uncomfortable life there. I was a free and gay young fellow in those days, (however much, sir, you may doubt the assertion, and think that I am changed), and not so particular in my choice of friends as subsequent experience has led me to be.

There lived in the set of Chambers opposite to mine, a Suffolk gentleman, of good family, whom I shall call Mr Bludyer. Our boys or clerks first made acquaintance, and did each other mutual kind offices: borrowing for their respective masters' benefit, neither of whom was too richly provided with the world's goods, coals, blacking brushes, crockery ware, and the like; and our forks and spoons, if either of us had an entertainment in Chambers. As I learned presently that Mr Bludyer had been educated at Oxford, and heard that his elder brother was a gentleman of good estate and reputation in his county, I could have no objection to make his acquaintance, and accepted finally his invitation to meet a large game pie which he had brought with him from the country, and I recollect I lent my own silver teapot, which figured handsomely on the occasion. It is the same one which I presented to you, when you took possession of your present apartments.

Mr Bludyer was a sporting man: it was the custom in those days with many gentlemen to dress as much like coachmen as possible: in top-boots, huge white coats with capes, Belcher neckerchiefs, and the like adornments; and at the tables of bachelors of the very first fashion, you would meet with prize fighters and jockeys, and hear a great deal about the prize ring, the cockpit, and the odds. I remember my Lord Tilbury was present at this breakfast, (who afterwards lamentably broke his neck in a steeple chase, by which the noble family became extinct), and for some time I confounded his lordship with Dutch Sam, who was also of the party, and, indeed, not unlike the noble Viscount in dress and manner.

My acquaintance with Mr Bludyer ripened into a sort of friendship. He was perfectly good-natured, and not ill-bred; and his jovial spirits and roaring stories amused a man who, though always of a peaceful turn, had no dislike to cheerful companions. We used to dine together at coffee houses, for Clubs were scarcely invented in those days, except for the aristocracy; and, in fine, were very intimate. Bludyer, a brave and athletic man, would often give a loose to his spirits of an evening, and mill a Charley or two, as the phrase then was.

The young bloods of those days thought it was no harm to spend a night in the watch-house, and I assure you it has accommodated a deal of good company. *Autres temps, autres moeurs.* In our own days, my good Bob, a station-house bench is not the bed for a gentleman.

I was at this time (and deservedly so, for I had been very kind to her, and my elder brother, your father, neglected her considerably) the favourite nephew of your grand-aunt, my aunt, Mrs General MacWhirter, who was left a very handsome fortune by the General, and to whom I do not scruple to confess I paid every attention to which her age, her sex, and her large income entitled her. I used to take sweetmeats to her poodle. I went and drank tea with her night after night. I accompanied her Sunday after Sunday to hear the Rev Rowland Hill, at the Rotunda Chapel, over Blackfriars Bridge, and I used to read many of the tracts with which she liberally supplied me – in fact, do everything to comfort and console a lady of peculiar opinions and habits who had a large jointure. Your father used to say I was a sneak, but he was then a boisterous young squire; and, perhaps, we were not particularly good friends.

Well, sir, my dear aunt, Mrs General MacWhirter, made me her chief confidant. I regulated her money matters for her, and acted with her bankers and lawyers; and as she always spoke of your father as a reprobate, I had every reason to suppose I should inherit the property, the main part of which passed to another branch of the Browns. I do not grudge it, Bob: I do not grudge it. Your family is large; and I have enough from my poor dear departed wife.

Now it so happened, that in June, 1811, – I recollect the Comet was blazing furiously at the time, and Mrs MacWhirter was of opinion that the world was at an end – Mr Bludyer, who was having his chambers in Pump Court painted, asked permission to occupy mine, where he wished to give a lunch to some people whom he was desirous to entertain. Thinking no harm, of course I said yes; and I went to my desk at the Tape and Sealing-Wax Office at my usual hour, giving instructions to my boy to make Mr Bludyer's friends comfortable.

As ill-luck would have it, on that accursed Friday, Mrs MacWhirter, who had never been up my staircase before in her life (for your dear grand-aunt was large in person, and the apoplexy which carried her off soon after menaced her always), having some very particular business with her solicitors in Middle Temple Lane, and being anxious to consult me about a mortgage, actually mounted my stairs, and opened the door on which she saw written the name of Mr Thomas Brown. She was a peculiar woman, I have said, attached to glaring colours in her dress, and from her long residence in India, seldom without a set of costly Birds of Paradise in her bonnet, and a splendid Cashmere shawl.

Fancy her astonishment then, on entering my apartments at three o'clock in the afternoon, to be assailed in the first place by a strong smell of tobacco smoke which pervaded the passage, and by a wild and ferocious bull-dog which flew at her on entering my sitting-room.

This bull-dog, sir, doubtless attracted by the brilliant colours of her costume, seized upon her, and pinned her down, screaming so that her voice drowned that of Bludyer himself, who was sitting on the table bellowing, 'A Southerly Wind and a Cloudy Sky proclaim it a Hunting Morning' – or some such ribald trash: and the brutal owner of the dog, (who was no other than the famous Mulatto boxer, Norroy, called the 'Black Prince' in the odious language of the Fancy, and who was inebriated doubtless at the moment), encouraged his dog in the assault upon this defenceless lady, and laughed at the agonies which she endured.

Mr Bludyer, the black man, and one or two more, were arranging a fight on Moulsey Hurst, when my poor aunt made her appearance among these vulgar wretches. Although it was but three o'clock, they had sent to a neighbouring tavern for gin-and-water, and the glasses sparkled on the board – to use a verse from a Bacchanalian song which I well remember Mr Bludyer used to yell forth – when I myself arrived from my office at my usual hour, half-past three. The black fellow and young Captain Cavendish of the Guards were the smokers; and it appears that at first all the gentlemen screamed with laughter; some of them called my aunt an 'old girl'; and it was not until she had nearly fainted that the filthy Mulatto called the dog off from the flounce of her yellow gown of which he had hold.

When this poor victim of vulgarity asked with a scream – Where was her nephew? new roars of laughter broke out from the coarse gin-drinkers. 'It's the old woman whom he goes to meeting with', cried out Bludyer. 'Come away, boys!' And he led his brutalized crew out of my chambers into his own, where they finished, no doubt, their arrangements about the fight.

Sir, when I came home at my usual hour of half-past three, I found Mrs MacWhirter in hysterics upon my sofa – the pipes were lying about – the tin-dish covers – the cold kidneys – the tavern cruet stands, and wretched remnants of the orgy were in disorder on the tablecloth, stained with beer. Seeing her fainting, I wildly bade my boy to open the window, and seizing a glass of water which was on the table, I presented it to her lips. – It was gin-and-water, which I proffered to that poor lady.

She started up with a scream, which terrified me so I upset the glass: and with empurpled features, and a voice quivering and choking with anger, she vowed she would never forgive me. In vain I pleaded that I was ignorant of the whole of these disgraceful transactions. I went down on my knees to her, and begged her to be pacified; I called my boy, and bade him bear witness to my innocence: the impudent young fiend burst out laughing in my face, and I kicked him downstairs as soon as she was gone: for go she did directly to her carriage, which was in waiting in Middle Temple Lane, and to which I followed her with tears in my eyes, amidst a crowd of jeering barristers' boys and Temple porters. But she pulled up the window in my face, and would no more come back to me than Eurydice would to Orpheus.

If I grow pathetic over this story, my dear Bob, have I not reason? Your great-aunt left thirty thousand pounds to your family, and the remainder to the missionaries, and it is a curious proof of the inconsistency of women, that she, a serious person, said on her deathbed that she would have left her money to me, if I had called out Mr Bludyer, who insulted her, and with whom I certainly would have exchanged shots, had I thought that Mrs MacWhirter would have encouraged any such murder.

My wishes, dear Bob, are moderate. Your aunt left me a handsome competency – and, I repeat, I do not grudge my brother George the money. Nor is it probable that such a calamity can happen again to any one of our family – that would be too great a misfortune. But I tell you the tale, because at least it shows you how important good company is, and that a young man about town should beware of his friends as well as of his enemies.

The other day I saw you walking by the Serpentine with young Lord Foozle, of the Windsor Heavies, who nodded to all sorts of suspicious broughams on the ride, while you looked about (you know you did, you young rascal) for acquaintances – as much as to say – 'See! here I am, Bob Brown, of Pump Court, walking with a lord.'

My dear Bob, I own that to walk with a lord, and to be seen with him, is a pleasant thing. Every man of the middle class likes to know persons of rank. If he says he don't – don't believe him. And I would certainly wish that you should associate with your superiors rather than your inferiors. There is no more dangerous or stupefying position for a man in life than to be a cock of small society. It prevents his ideas from growing: it renders him intolerably conceited. A twopenny halfpenny Caesar, a Brummagem dandy, a coterie philosopher or wit, is pretty sure to be an ass; and, in fine, I set it down as a maxim that it is good for a man to live where he can meet his betters, intellectual and social.

But if you fancy that getting into Lord Foozle's set will do you good or advance your prospects in life, my dear Bob, you are wofully mistaken. The Windsor Heavies are a most gentleman-like, well-made, and useful set of men. The conversation of such of them as I have had the good fortune to meet, has not certainly inspired me with a respect for their intellectual qualities, nor is their life commonly of that kind which rigid ascetics would pronounce blameless. Some of the young men amongst them talk to the broughams, frequent the private boxes, dance at the Casinos; few read – many talk about horseflesh and the odds after dinner, or relax with a little lansquenet or a little billiards at Pratt's.

My boy, it is not with the eye of a moralist that your venerable old uncle examines these youths, but rather of a natural philosopher, who inspects them as he would any other phenomenon, or queer bird, or odd fish, or fine flower. These fellows are like the flowers, and neither toil nor spin, but are decked out in magnificent apparel: and for some wise and useful purpose no doubt. It is good that there should be honest, handsome, hard-living, hard-riding, stupid young Windsor Heavies – as that there should be polite young gentlemen in the Temple, or any other variety of our genus.

And it is good that you should go from time to time to the Heavies' mess, if they ask you; and know that worthy set of gentlemen. But beware, O Bob, how you live with them. Remember that your lot in life is to toil, and spin too – and calculate how much time it takes a Heavy or a man of that condition to do nothing. Say, he dines at eight o'clock, and spends seven hours after dinner in pleasure. Well, if he goes to bed at three in the morning – that precious youth must have nine hours' sleep, which bring him to twelve o'clock next day, when he will have a headache probably, so that he can hardly be expected to dress, rally, have devilled chicken and pale ale, and get out before three. Friendship – the Club – the visits which he is compelled to pay, occupy him till five or six, and what time is there left for exercise and a ride in the Park, and for a second toilette preparatory to dinner, &c.? – He goes on his routine of pleasure, this young Heavy, as you on yours of duty – one man in London is pretty nearly as busy as another. The company of young 'Swells', then, if you will permit me the word, is not for you. You must consider that you should not spend more than a certain sum for your dinner – they need not. You wear a black coat, and they a shining cuirass and monstrous epaulets. Yours is the useful part in life and theirs the splendid – though why speak further on this subject? Since the days of the Frog and the Bull, a desire to cope with Bulls has been known to be fatal to Frogs.

And to know young noblemen, and brilliant and notorious town bucks and leaders of fashion, has this great disadvantage – that if you talk about them or are seen with them much, you offend all your friends of middle life. It makes men angry to see their acquaintances better off than they themselves are. If you live much with great people, others will be sure to say that you are a sneak. I have known Jack Jolliff, whose fun and spirits made him adored by the dandies (for they are just such folks as you and I, only with not quite such good brains, and perhaps better manners – simple folks who want to be amused – I have known Jack Jolliff, I say, offend a whole roomful of men by telling us that he had been dining with a Duke. *We* hadn't been to dine with a Duke. We were not courted by grandees – and we disliked the man who was, and said he was a parasite, because men of fashion courted him. I don't know any means by which men hurt themselves more in the estimation of their equals than this of talking of great folks. A man may mean no harm by it – he speaks of the grandees with whom he lives, as you and I do of Jack and Tom who give us dinners. But his old acquaintances do not forgive him his superiority, and set the Tuft-hunted down as the Tuft-hunter.

I remember laughing at the jocular complaint made by one of this sort, a friend, whom I shall call Main. After Main published his 'Travels in the Libyan Desert' four years ago, he became a literary lion, and roared in many of the metropolitan *salons*. He is a good natured fellow, never in the least puffed up by his literary success; and always said that it would not last. His greatest leonine quality, however, is his appetite; and to behold him engaged on a Club joint, or to see him make away with pounds of turbot, and plate after plate of *entrées*, roasts, and sweets, is indeed a remarkable sight, and refreshing to those who like to watch animals feeding. But since Main has gone out of, and other authors have come into, fashion – the poor fellow comically grumbles. 'That year of lionization has ruined me. The people who used to ask me before, don't ask me any more. They are afraid to invite me to Bloomsbury, because they fancy I am accustomed to Mayfair, and Mayfair has long since taken up with a new roarer – so that I am quite alone!' And thus he dines at the Club almost every day at his own charges now, and attacks the joint. I do not envy the man who comes after him to the haunch of mutton.

If Fate, then, my dear Bob, should bring you in contact with a lord or two, eat their dinners, enjoy their company, but be mum about them when you go away.

And, though it is a hard and cruel thing to say, I would urge you, my dear Bob, specially to beware of taking pleasant fellows for your friends. Choose a good disagreeable friend, if you be wise – a surly, steady, economical, rigid fellow. All jolly fellows, all delights of Club smoking-rooms and billiard rooms, all fellows who sing a capital song, and the like, are sure to be poor. As they are free with their own money, so will they be with yours; and their very generosity and goodness of disposition will prevent them from having the means of paying you back. They lend their money to some other jolly fellows. They accommodate each other by putting their jolly names to the backs of jolly bills. Gentlemen in Cursitor Street are on the lookout for them. Their tradesmen ask for them, and find them not. Ah! Bob, it's hard times with a gentleman, when he has to walk round a street for fear of meeting a creditor there, and for a man of courage, when he can't look a tailor in the face.

Eschew jolly fellows then, my boy, as the most dangerous and costly of company; and àpropos of bills – if I ever hear of your putting your name to stamped paper – I will disown you, and cut you off with a protested shilling.

I know many men who say (whereby I have my private opinion of their own probity) that all poor people are dishonest: this is a hard word, though more generally true than some folks suppose – but I fear that all people much in debt are not honest. A man who has to wheedle a tradesman is not going through a very honourable business in life – a man with a bill becoming due tomorrow morning, and putting a good face on it in the Club, is perforce a hypocrite whilst he is talking to you – a man who has to do any meanness about money I fear he is so nearly like a rogue, that it's not much use calculating where the difference lies. Let us be very gentle with our neighbours' failings and forgive our friends their debts, as we hope ourselves to be forgiven. But the best thing of all to do with your debts is to pay them. Make none; and don't live with people who do. Why, if I dine with a man who is notoriously living beyond his means, I am a hypocrite certainly myself, and I fear a bit of a rogue too. I try to make my host believe that I believe him an honest fellow. I look his sham splendour in the face without saying, 'You are an impostor.' – Alas, Robert, I have partaken of feasts where it seemed to me that the plate, the viands, the wine, the servants, and butlers, were all sham, like Cinderella's coach and footmen, and would turn into rats and mice, and an old shoe or a cabbage stalk, as soon as we were out of the house and the clock struck twelve.

MR BROWN THE ELDER TAKES MR BROWN THE YOUNGER TO A CLUB

I

Presuming that my dear Bobby would scarcely consider himself to be an accomplished man about town, until he had obtained an entrance into a respectable Club, I am happy to inform you that you are this day elected a Member of the 'Polyanthus', having been proposed by my friend, Lord Viscount Colchicum, and seconded by your affectionate uncle. I have settled with Mr Stiff, the worthy Secretary, the preliminary pecuniary arrangements regarding the entrance fee and the first annual subscription – the ensuing payments I shall leave to my worthy nephew.

You were elected, sir, with but two black balls; and every other man who was put up for ballot had four, with the exception of Tom Harico, who had more black beans than white. Do not, however, be puffed up by this victory, and fancy yourself more popular than other men. Indeed I don't mind telling you (but, of course, I do not wish it to go any further), that Captain Slyboots and I, having suspicions of the meeting, popped a couple of adverse balls into the candidate's boxes; so that, at least, you should, in case of mishap, not be unaccompanied in ill fortune.

Now, then, that you are a member of the 'Polyanthus', I trust you will comport yourself with propriety in the place; and permit me to offer you a few hints with regard to your bearing.

We are not so stiff at the 'Polyanthus' as at some clubs I could name – and a good deal of decent intimacy takes place amongst us. – Do not therefore enter the Club, as I have seen men do at the 'Chokers' (of which I am also a member), with your eyes scowling under your hat at your neighbour, and with an expression of countenance which seems to say, 'Hang your impudence, sir. How dare you stare at *me*?' Banish that absurd dignity and swagger, which do not at all become your youthful countenance, my dear Bob, and let us walk up the steps and into the place. See, old Noseworthy is in the bow-window reading the paper – he is always in the bow-window reading the paper.

We pass by the worthy porter, and alert pages – a fifteen-hundredth part of each of whom is henceforth your paid for property – and you see he takes down your name as Mr R. Brown, Junior, and will know you and be civil to you until death – Ha, there is Jawkins, as usual; he has nailed poor Styles up against a pillar, and is telling him what the opinion of the City is about George Hudson, Esq, and when Sir Robert will take the government. How d'you do, Jawkins? – Satisfactory news from India? Gilbert to be made Baron Gilbert of Goojerat? Indeed, I don't introduce you to Jawkins, my poor Bob; he will do that for himself, and you will have quite enough of him before many days are over.

Those three gentlemen sitting on the sofa are from our beloved sister island; they come here every day, and wait for the Honourable Member for Ballinafad, who is at present in the writing room.

I have remarked, in London, however, that every Irish gentleman is accompanied by other Irish gentlemen, who wait for him as here, or at the corner of the street. These are waiting until the Honourable Member for Ballinafad can get them three places, in the Excise, in the Customs, and a little thing in the Post Office, no doubt. One of them sends home a tremendous account of parties and politics here, which appears in the *Ballinafad Banner*. He knows everything. He has just been closeted with Peel, and can vouch for it that Clarendon has been sent for. He knows who wrote the famous pamphlet, 'Ways and Means for Ireland', – all the secrets of the present Cabinet, the designs of Sir James Graham. How Lord John can live under those articles which he writes in the *Banner* is a miracle to me! I hope he will get that little thing in the Post Office soon.

This is the newspaper room – enter the Porter with the evening papers – what a rush the men make for them! Do you want to see one? Here is the *Standard* – nice article about the 'Starling Club' – very pleasant, candid, gentleman-like notice – Club composed of clergymen, atheists, authors, and artists. Their chief conversation is blasphemy: they have statues of Socrates and Mahomet on the centre piece of the dinner-table, take every opportunity of being disrespectful to Moses, and a dignified clergyman always proposes the Glorious, Pious, and Immortal Memory of Confucius. Grace is said backwards, and the Catechism treated with the most irreverent ribaldry by the comic authors and the general company. – Are these men to be allowed to meet, and their horrid orgies to continue? Have you had enough? – let us go into the other rooms.

What a calm and pleasant seclusion the library presents after the bawl and bustle of the newspaper room? There is never anybody here. English gentlemen get up such a prodigious quantity of knowledge in their early life, that they leave off reading soon after they begin to shave, or never look at anything but a newspaper. How pleasant this room is, – isn't it? with its sober draperies, and long calm lines of peaceful volumes – nothing to interrupt the quiet – only the melody of Horner's nose as he lies asleep upon one of the sofas. What is he reading? Hah! 'Pendennis', No. VII, hum, let us pass on. Have you read 'David Copperfield', by the way? How beautiful it is – how charmingly fresh and simple! In those admirable touches of tender humour – and I should call humour, Bob, a mixture of love and wit – who can equal this great genius? There are little words and phrases in his books which are like personal benefits to the reader. What a place it is to hold in the affections of men! What an awful responsibility hanging over a writer! What man holding such a place, and knowing that his words go forth to vast congregations of mankind, – to grown folks – to their children, and perhaps to their children's children, – but must think of his calling with a solemn and humble heart! May love and truth guide such a man always! It is an awful prayer; may heaven further its fulfilment! And then, Bob, let the *Record* revile him – See, here's Horner waking up – How do you do, Horner?

This neighbouring room, which is almost as quiet as the library, is the card room, you see. There are always three or four devotees assembled in it; and the lamps are scarcely ever out in this Temple of Trumps.

I admire, as I see them, my dear Bobby, grave and silent at these little green tables, not moved outwardly by grief or pleasure at losing or winning, but calmly pursuing their game (as that pursuit is called, which is in fact the most elaborate science and study) at noonday, entirely absorbed, and philosophically indifferent to the bustle and turmoil of the enormous working world without. Disraeli may make his best speech; the Hungarians may march into Vienna; the Protectionists come in; Louis Philippe be restored; or the Thames set on fire; and Colonel Pam and Mr Trumpington will never leave their table, so engaging is their occupation at it. The turning up of an ace is of more interest to them than all the affairs of all the world besides – and so they will go on until Death summons them, and their last trump is played.

It is curious to think that a century ago almost all gentlemen, soldiers, statesmen, men of science, and divines, passed hours at play every day; as our grandmothers did likewise. The poor old kings and queens must feel the desertion now, and deplore the present small number of their worshippers, as compared to the myriads of faithful subjects who served them in past times.

I do not say that other folks' pursuits are much more or less futile; but fancy a life such as that of the Colonel – eight or nine hours of sleep, eight of trumps, and the rest for business, reading, exercise, and domestic duty or affection (to be sure he's most likely a bachelor, so that the latter offices do not occupy him much) – fancy such a life, and at its conclusion at the age of seventy-five, the worthy gentleman being able to say, I have spent twenty-five years of my existence turning up trumps.

With Trumpington matters are different. Whist is a profession with him, just as much as Law is yours. He makes the deepest study of it – he makes every sacrifice to his pursuit: he may be fond of wine and company, but he eschews both, to keep his head cool and play his rubber. He is a man of good parts, and was once well read, as you see by his conversation when he is away from the table, but he gives up reading for play – and knows that to play well a man must play every day. He makes three or four hundred a year by his Whist, and well he may – with his brains, and half his industry, he could make a larger income at any other profession.

In a game with these two gentlemen, the one who has been actually seated at that card table for a term as long as your whole life, the other who is known as a consummate practitioner, do you think it is likely you will come off a winner? The state of your fortune is your lookout, not theirs. They are there at their posts – like knights ready to meet all comers. If you choose to engage them, sit down. They will, with the most perfect probity, calmness, and elegance of manner, win and win of you until they have won every shilling of a fortune, when they will make you a bow, and wish you good morning. You may go and drown yourself afterwards – it is not their business. Their business is to be present in that room, and to play cards with you or anybody. When you are done with – *Bon jour*. My dear Colonel, let me introduce you to a new member, my nephew, Mr Robert Brown.

The other two men at the table are the Honourable G. Windgall and Mr Chanter: perhaps you have not heard that the one made rather a queer settlement at the last Derby; and the other has just issued from one of her Majesty's establishments in St George's Fields.

Either of these gentlemen is perfectly affable, good natured, and easy of access – and will cut you for half-crowns if you like, or play you at any game on the cards. They descend from their broughams or from horseback at the Club door with the most splendid air, and they feast upon the best dishes and wines in the place.

But do you think it advisable to play cards with them? Which know the games best – you or they? Which are most likely – we will not say to play foul – but to take certain little advantages in the game which their consummate experience teaches them – you or they? Finally, is it a matter of perfect certainty, if you won, that they would pay you?

Let us leave these gentlemen, my dear Bob, and go through the rest of the house.

MR BROWN THE ELDER TAKES MR BROWN THE YOUNGER TO A CLUB

II

rom the library we proceed to the carved and gilded drawing-room of the Club, the damask hangings of which are embroidered with our lovely emblem, the Polyanthus, and which is fitted with a perfectly unintelligible splendour. Sardanapalus, if he had pawned one of his kingdoms, could not have had such mirrors as one of those in which I see my dear Bob admiring the tie of his cravat with such complacency, and I am sure I cannot comprehend why Smith and Brown should have their persons reflected in such vast sheets of quicksilver; or why, if we have a mind to a sixpenny cup of tea and muffins, when we come in with muddy boots from a dirty walk, those refreshments should be served to us as we occupy a sofa much more splendid, and far better stuffed, than any Louis Quatorze ever sat upon. I want a sofa, as I want a friend, upon which I can repose familiarly. If you can't have intimate terms and freedom with one and the other, they are of no good. A full-dress Club is an absurdity – and no man ought to come into this room except in a uniform or court suit. I daren't put my feet on younder sofa for fear of sullying the damask, or worse still, for fear that Hicks the Committee-man should pass, and spy out my sacrilegious boots on the cushion.

We pass through these double-doors, and enter rooms of a very different character.

By the faint and sickly odour pervading this apartment, by the opened windows, by the circular stains upon the marble tables, which indicate the presence of brandies-and-waters long passed into the world of spirits, my dear Bob will have no difficulty in recognizing the smoking-room, where I dare say he will pass a good deal of his valuable time henceforth.

If I could recommend a sure way of advancement and profit to a young man about town, it would be, after he has come away from a friend's house and dinner, where he has to a surety had more than enough of claret and good things, when he ought to be going to bed at midnight, so that he might rise fresh and early for his morning's work, to stop, nevertheless, for a couple of hours at the Club, and smoke in this room and tipple weak brandy-and-water.

By a perseverance in this system, you may get a number of advantages. By sitting up till three of a summer morning, you have the advantage of seeing the sunrise, and as you walk home to Pump Court, can mark the quiet of the streets in the rosy glimmer of the dawn. You can easily spend in that smoking-room, (as for the billiard room adjacent, how much more can't you get rid of there), and without any inconvenience or extravagance whatever, enough money to keep you a horse. Three or four cigars when you are in the Club, your case filled when you are going away, a couple of glasses of very weak cognac and cold water, will cost you sixty pounds a year, as sure as your name is Bob Brown. And as for the smoking and tippling, plus billiards, they may be made to cost anything.

And then you have the advantage of hearing such delightful and instructive conversation in a Club smoking-room, between the hours of twelve and three! Men who frequent that place at that hour are commonly men of studious habits and philosophical and reflective minds, to whose opinions it is pleasant and profitable to listen. They are full of anecdotes, which are always moral and well-chosen; their talk is never free, or on light subjects. I have one or two old smoking-room pillars in my eye now, who would be perfect models for any young gentleman entering life, and to whom a father could not do better than entrust the education of his son.

To drop the satirical vein, my dear Bob, I am compelled as a man to say my opinion, that the best thing you can do with regard to that smoking-room is to keep out of it; or at any rate never to be seen in the place after midnight. They are very pleasant and frank, those jolly fellows, those loose fishes, those fast young men – but the race in life is not to such fast men as these – and you who want to win must get up early of a morning, my boy. You and an old college chum or two may sit together over your cigar boxes in one another's chambers, and talk till all hours, and do yourselves good probably. Talking among you is a wholesome exercitation; humour comes in an easy flow; it doesn't preclude grave argument and manly interchange of thought – I own myself, when I was younger, to have smoked many a pipe with advantage in the company of Doctor Parr. Honest men, with pipes or cigars in their mouths, have great physical advantages in conversation. You may stop talking if you like – but the breaks of silence never seem disagreeable, being filled up by the puffing of the smoke – hence there is no awkwardness in resuming the conversation – no straining for effect – sentiments are delivered in a grave easy manner – the cigar harmonizes the society, and soothes at once the speaker and the subject whereon he converses. I have no doubt that it is from the habit of smoking that Turks and American-Indians are such monstrous well-bred men. The pipe draws wisdom from the lips of the philosopher, and shuts up the mouth of the foolish: it generates a style of conversation, contemplative, thoughtful, benevolent, and unaffected: in fact, dear Bob, I must out with it – I am an old smoker. At home I have done it up the chimney rather than not do it (the which I own is a crime). I vow and believe that the cigar has been one of the greatest creature-comforts of my life – a kind companion, a gentle stimulant, an amiable anodyne, a cementer of friendship. May I die if I abuse that kindly weed which has given me so much pleasure!

Since I have been a member of that Club, what numbers of men have occupied this room and departed from it, like so many smoked-out cigars, leaving nothing behind but a little disregarded ashes! Bob, my boy, they drop off in the course of twenty years, our boon companions, and jolly fellow bottle-crackers. – I mind me of many a good fellow who has talked and laughed here, and whose pipe is put out for ever. Men, I remember as dashing youngsters but the other day, have passed into the state of old fogies: they have sons, sir, of almost your age, when first we joined the 'Polyanthus'. Grass grows over others in all parts of the world. Where is poor Ned? Where is poor Fred? Dead rhymes with Ned and Fred too – their place knows them not – their names one year appeared at the end of the Club list, under the dismal category of 'Members Deceased', in which you and I shall rank some day. Do you keep that subject steadily in your mind? I do not see why one shouldn't meditate upon Death in Pall Mall as well as in a howling wilderness. There is enough to remind one of it at every corner. There is a strange face looking out of Jack's old lodgings in Jermyn Street – somebody else has got the Club chair which Tom used to occupy. He doesn't dine here and grumble as he used formerly. He has been sent for, and has not come back again – one day Fate will send for us, and we shall not return – and the people will come down to the Club as usual, saying, 'Well, and so poor old Brown is gone.' – Indeed, a smoking-room on a morning is not a cheerful spot.

Our room has a series of tenants of quite distinct characters. After an early and sober dinner below, certain *habitués* of the 'Polyanthus' mount up to this apartment for their coffee and cigar, and talk as gravely as Sachems at a Palaver. Trade and travel, politics and geography, and their discourse – they are in bed long before their successors the jolly fellows begin their night life, and the talk of the one set is as different to the conversation of the other, as any talk can be.

After the grave old Sachems, come other frequenters of the room; a squad of sporting men very likely – very solemn and silent personages these – who give the odds, and talk about the Cup in a darkling undertone. Then you shall have three or four barristers with high voices, seldom able to sit long without talking of their profession, or mentioning something about Westminster Hall. About eleven, men in white neckcloths drop in from dinner parties, and show their lacquered boots and shirt-studs with a little complacency – and at midnight, after the theatres, the young rakes and *viveurs* come swaggering in, and call loudly for gin-twist.

But as for a Club smoking-room after midnight, I vow again that you are better out of it: that you will waste money and your precious hours and health there; and you may frequent this 'Polyanthus' room for a year, and not carry away from the place one single idea or story that can do you the least good in life. How much you shall take away of another sort, I do not here set down; but I have before my mind's eye the image of old Silenus, with purple face and chalk-stone fingers, telling his foul old garrison legends over his gin-and-water. He is in the smoking-room every night; and I feel that no one can get benefit from the society of that old man.

What society he has he gets from this place. He sits for hours in a corner of the sofa, and makes up his parties here. He will ask you after a little time, seeing that you are a gentleman and have a good address, and will give you an exceedingly good dinner. I went once, years ago, to a banquet of his – and found all the men at his table were Polyanthuses: so that it was a house dinner in — Square, with Mrs Silenus at the head of the table.

After dinner she retired and was no more seen, and Silenus amused himself by making poor Mr Tippleton drunk. He came to the Club the next day, he amused himself by describing the arts by which he had practised upon the easy brains of poor Mr Tippleton – (as if that poor fellow wanted any arts or persuasion to induce him to intoxicate himself), and told all the smoking-room how he had given a dinner, how many bottles of wine had been emptied, and how many Tippleton had drunk for his share. 'I kept my eye on Tip, sir,' the horrid old fellow said – 'I took care to make him mix his liquors well, and before eleven o'clock I finished him, and had him as drunk as a lord, sir!' Will you like to have that gentleman for a friend? He has elected himself our smoking-room king at the 'Polyanthus', and midnight monarch.

As he talks, in comes poor Tippleton – a kind soul – a gentleman – a man of reading and parts – who has friends at home very likely and had once a career before him – and what is he now? His eyes are vacant; he reels into a sofa corner, and sits in maudlin silence, and hiccups every now and then. Old Silenus winks knowingly round at the whole smoking-room: most of the men sneer – some pity – some very young cubs laugh and jeer at him. Tippleton's drunk.

III

From the Library and smoking-room regions let us descend to the lower floor. Here you behold the coffee-room, where the neat little tables are already laid out, awaiting the influx of diners.

A great advance in civilization was made, and the honesty as well as economy of young men of the middle classes immensely promoted, when the ancient tavern system was overthrown, and those houses of meeting instituted where a man, without sacrificing his dignity, could dine for a couple of shillings. I remember in the days of my youth when a very moderate dinner at a reputable coffee-house cost a man half-a-guinea: when you were obliged to order a pint of wine for the good of the house; when the waiter got a shilling for his attendance; and when young gentlemen were no richer than they are now, and had to pay thrice as much as they at present need to disburse for the maintenance of their station.

Then men (who had not the half-guinea at command) used to dive into dark streets in the vicinage of Soho or Covent Garden, and get a meagre meal at shilling taverns – or Tom, the clerk, issued out from your Chambers in Pump Court and brought back your dinner between two plates from a neighbouring ham-and-beef shop. Either repast was strictly honourable, and one can find no earthly fault with a poor gentleman for eating a poor meal. But that solitary meal in Chambers was indeed a dismal refection. I think with anything but regret of those lonely feasts of beef and cabbage; and how there was no resource for the long evenings but those books, over which you had been poring all day, or the tavern with its deuced expenses, or the theatre with its vicious attractions. A young bachelor's life was a clumsy piece of wretchedness then – mismanaged and ill economized – just as your Temple Chambers or College rooms now are, which are quite behind the age in the decent conveniences which every modern tenement possesses.

And that dining for a shilling and strutting about Pall Mall afterwards was, after all, an hypocrisy. At the time when the 'Trois Frères Provençaux' at Paris had two entrances, one into the place of the Palais Royal, and one into the street behind, where the sixteen-sous dinner-houses are, I have seen bucks with profuse toothpicks walk out of these latter houses of entertainment, pass up the 'Trois Frères' stairs, and descend from the other door into the Palais Royal, so that the people walking there might fancy these poor fellows had been dining regardless of expense. No; what you call putting a good face upon poverty, that is, hiding it under a grin, or concealing its rags under a makeshift, is always rather a base stratagem. Your Beaux Tibbs and twopenny dandies can never be respectable altogether; and if a man is poor, I say he ought to seem poor; and that both he and Society are in the wrong, if either sees any cause of shame in poverty.

That is why we ought to be thankful for Clubs. Here is no skulking to get a cheap dinner; no ordering of expensive liquors and dishes for the good of the house, or cowering sensitiveness as to the opinion of the waiter. We advance in simplicity and honesty as we advance in civilization, and it is my belief that we become better bred and less artificial, and tell more truth every day.

This, you see, is the Club coffee-room – it is three o'clock; young Wideawake is just finishing his breakfast (with whom I have nothing to do at present, but to say parenthetically, that if you *will* sit up till five o'clock in the morning, Bob my boy, you may look out to have a headache and a breakfast at three in the afternoon). Wideawake is at breakfast – Goldsworthy is ordering his dinner – while Mr Nudgit, whom you see yonder, is making his lunch. In those two gentlemen is the moral and exemplification of the previous little remarks which I have been making.

You must know, sir, that at the 'Polyanthus', in common with most Clubs, gentlemen are allowed to enjoy, gratis, in the a Coffee-room, bread, beer, sauces, and pickles.

After four o'clock, if you order your dinner, you have to pay sixpence for what is called the table – the clean cloth, the vegetables, cheese, and so forth: before that hour you may have lunch, when there is no table charge.

Now, Goldsworthy is a gentleman and a man of genius, who has courage and simplicity enough to be poor – not like some fellows whom one meets, and who make a *fanfaronnade* of poverty, and draping themselves in their rags, seem to cry, 'See how virtuous I am, – how honest Diogenes is!' but he is a very poor man, whose education and talents are of the best, and who in so far claims to rank with the very best people in the world. In his place in Parliament, when he takes off his hat (which is both old and well brushed), the Speaker's eye is pretty sure to meet his, and the House listens to him with the respect which is due to so much honesty and talent. He is the equal of any man, however lofty or wealthy. His social position is rather improved by his poverty, and the world, which is a manly and generous world in its impulses, however it may be in its practice, contemplates with a sincere regard and admiration Mr Goldsworthy's manner of bearing his lack of fortune. He is going to dine for a shilling; he will have two mutton chops (and the mutton chop is a thing unknown in domestic life and in the palaces of epicures, where you may get cutlets dressed with all sorts of French sauces, but not the admirable mutton chop), and with a due allowance of the

Club bread and beer, he will make a perfectly wholesome, and sufficient, and excellent meal; and go down to the House and fire into Ministers this very night.

Now, I say, this man dining for a shilling is a pleasant spectacle to behold. I respect Mr Goldsworthy with all my heart, without sharing those ultra-conservative political opinions which we all know he entertains, and from which no interest, temptation, or hope of place will cause him to swerve: and you see he is waited upon with as much respect here as old Silenus, though he order the most sumptuous banquet the cook can devise, or bully the waiters ever so.

But ah, Bob! what can we say of the conduct of that poor little Mr Nudgit? He has a bed chamber in some court unknown in the neighbourhood of the 'Polyanthus'. He makes a breakfast with the Club bread and beer; he lunches off the same supplies – and being of an Epicurean taste, look what he does – he is actually pouring a cruet of anchovy sauce over his bread to give it a flavour; and I have seen the unconscionable little gourmand sidle off to the pickle jars when he thought nobody was observing, and pop a walnut or half a dozen of pickled onions into his mouth, and swallow them with a hideous furtive relish.

He disappears at dinner-time, and returns at half-past seven or eight o'clock, and wanders round the tables when the men are at their dessert and generous over their wine. He has a number of little stories about the fashionable world to tell, and is not unentertaining. When you dine here, sometimes give Nudgit a glass or two out of your decanter, Bob my boy, and comfort his poor old soul. He was a gentleman once and had money, as he will be sure to tell you. He is mean and feeble, but not unkind – a poor little parasite not to be unpitied. Mr Nudgit, allow me to introduce you to a new member, my nephew, Mr Robert Brown.

At this moment, old Silenus swaggers in, bearing his great waistcoat before him, and walking up to the desk where the coffee-room clerk sits and where the bills of fare are displayed. As he passes, he has to undergo the fire of Mr Goldsworthy's eyes, which dart out at him two flashes of the most killing scorn. He has passed by the battery without sinking, and lays himself alongside the desk. Nudgit watches him, and will presently go up smirking humbly to join him.

'Hunt,' he says, 'I want a table, my table, you know, at seven – dinner for eight – Lord Hobanob dines with me – send the butler – What's in the bill of fare? Let's have clear soup and turtle – I've sent it in from the City – dressed fish and turbot,' and with a swollen trembling hand he writes down a pompous bill of fare.

As I said, Nudgit comes up simpering, with a newspaper in his hand.

'Hullo, Nudg!' says Mr Silenus, 'how's the beer? Pickles good today?'

Nudgit smiles in a gentle deprecatory manner.

'Smell out a good dinner, hey, Nudg?' says Dives.

'If any man knows how to give one, you do,' answers the poor beggar. 'I wasn't a bad hand at ordering a dinner myself, once; what's the fish in the list today?' and with a weak smile he casts his eye over the bill of fare.

'Lord Hobanob dines with me, and *he* knows what a good dinner is, I can tell you,' says Mr Silenus, 'so does Cramley.'

'Both well-known epicures,' says Nudgit.

'I'm going to give Hobanob a return dinner to his at the 'Rhododendrum'. He bet me that Batifol the *chef* at the 'Rhododendrum' did better than our man can. Hob's dinner was last Wednesday, and I don't say it wasn't a good one; or that taking Grosbois by surprise, is giving him quite fair play – but we'll see, Nudgit. *I* know what Grosbois can do.'

'I should think you did, indeed, Silenus,' says the other.

'I see your mouth's watering. I'd ask you, only I know you're engaged. You're always engaged, Nudgit – not today? Well then, you may come; and I say, Mr Nudgit, we'll have a wet evening, sir, mind you that.'

Mr Bowls, the butler, here coming in, Mr Silenus falls into conversation with him about wines and icing. I am glad poor Nudgit has got his dinner. He will go and walk in the Park to get up an appetite. And now, Mr Bob, having shown you over your new house, I too will bid you for the present farewell.

A WORD ABOUT BALLS IN SEASON

hen my good friend, *Mr Punch*, sometime since, asked me to compile a series of conversations for young men in the dancing world, so that they might be agreeable to their partners, and advance their own success in life, I consented with a willing heart to my venerable friend's request, for I desire nothing better than to promote the amusement and happiness of all young people; and nothing, I thought, would be easier than to touch off a few light, airy, graceful little sets of phrases, which young fellows might adopt or expand, according to their own ingenuity and leisure.

Well, sir, I imagined myself, just for an instant, to be young again, and that I had a neat waist instead of that bow-window with which Time and Nature have ornamented the castle of my body, and brown locks instead of a bald pate (there was a time, sir, when my hair was not considered the worst part of me, and I recollect when I was a young man in the Militia, and when pigtails finally went out in our corps, who it was that longed to have my *queue* – it was found in her desk at her death, and my poor dear wife was always jealous of her), – I just chose, I say, to fancy myself a young man, and that I

47

would go up in imagination and ask a girl to dance with me. So I chose Maria – a man might go farther and fare worse than choose Maria, Mr Bob.

'My dear Miss E,' says I, 'may I have the honour of dancing the next set with you?'

'The next *what*?' says Miss E, smiling, and turning to Mrs E., as if to ask what a set meant.

'I forgot,' says I; 'the next quadrille, I would say.'

'It is rather slow dancing quadrilles,' says Miss E; 'but if I must, I must.'

'Well, then, a waltz, will that do? I know nothing prettier than a waltz played not too quick.'

'What!' says she, 'do you want a horrid old three-timed waltz, like that which the little figures dance upon the barrel organs? You silly old creature: you are good natured, but you are in your dotage. All these dances are passed away. You might as well ask me to wear a gown with a waist up to my shoulders, like that in which mamma was married; or a hoop and high heels, like grandmamma in the picture; or to dance a gavotte or a minuet. Things are changed, old gentleman – the fashions of your time are gone, and – and the bucks of your time will go too, Mr Brown. If I want to dance, here is Captain Whiskerfield, who is ready; or young Studdington, who is a delightful partner. He brings a little animation into our balls; and when he is not in society, dances every night at Vauxhall and the Casino.'

I pictured to myself Maria giving some such reply to my equally imaginative demand – for of course I never made the request, any more than she did the answer – and in fact, dear Bob, after turning over the matter of ballroom conversations in my mind, and sitting with pen and ink before me for a couple of hours, I found that I had nothing at all to say on the subject, and have no more right to teach a youth what he is to say in the present day to his partner, than I should have had in my own boyhood to instruct my own grandmother in the art of sucking eggs. We should pay as much reverence to youth as we should to age; there are points in which you young folks are altogether our superiors: and I can't help constantly crying out to persons of my own years, when busied about their young people – leave them alone; don't be always meddling

with their affairs, which they can manage for themselves;
don't be always insisting upon managing their boats, and
putting your oars in the water with theirs.

So I have the modesty to think that *Mr Punch* and I were a
couple of conceited old fogies, in devising the above plan of
composing conversation for the benefit of youth, and that
young folks can manage to talk of what interests them,
without any prompting on our part. To say the truth, I have
hardly been to a ball these three years. I saw the head of the
stair at H E's the T—— Ambassador in Br——ne Square, the
other night, but retired without even getting a sight of, or
making my bow to Her Excellency; thinking wisely that *mon
lait de poule et mon bonnet de nuit* much better became me at that
hour of midnight than the draught in a crowded passage, and
the sight of ever so many beauties.

But though I don't go myself to these assemblies, I have
intelligence amongst people who go: and hear from the girls
and their mammas what they do, and how they enjoy
themselves. I must own that some of the new arrangements
please me very much, as being natural and simple, and, in so
far, superior to the old mode.

In my time, for instance, a ballroom used to be more than
half-filled with old male and female fogies, whose persons
took up a great deal of valuable room, who did not in the least
ornament the walls against which they stood, and who would
have been much better at home in bed. In a great country
house, where you have a hall fireplace in which an ox might be
roasted conveniently, the presence of a few score more or less
of stout old folks can make no difference; there is room for
them at the card tables, and round the supper board, and the
sight of their honest red faces and white waistcoats lining the
wall cheers and illuminates the Assembly Room.

But it is a very different case when you have a small house in
Mayfair, or in the pleasant district of Pimlico and Tyburn; and
accordingly I am happy to hear that the custom is rapidly
spreading of asking none but dancing people to balls. It was
only this morning that I was arguing the point with our cousin
Mrs Crowder, who was greatly irate because her daughter
Fanny had received an invitation to go with her aunt, Mrs
Timmins, to Lady Tutbury's ball, whereas poor Mrs Crowder

had been told that she could on no account get a card.

Now Blanche Crowder is a very large woman naturally, and with the present fashion of flounces in dress, this balloon of a creature would occupy the best part of a little back drawing-room; whereas Rosa Timmins is a little bit of a thing, who takes up no space at all, and furnishes the side of a room as prettily as a bank of flowers could. I tried to convince our cousin upon this point, this *embonpoint*, I may say, and of course being too polite to make remarks personal to Mrs Crowder, I playfully directed them elsewhere.

'Dear Blanche,' said I, 'don't you see how greatly Lady Tutbury would have to extend her premises if all the relatives of all her dancers were to be invited? She has already flung out a marquee over the leads, and actually included the cistern – what can she do more? If all the girls were to have chaperons, where could the elders sit? Tutbury himself will not be present. He is a large and roomy man, like your humble servant, and Lady Tut has sent him off to Greenwich, or the 'Star and Garter' for the night, where, I have no doubt, he and some other stout fellows will make themselves comfortable. At a ball amongst persons of moderate means and large acquaintance in London, room is much more precious than almost anybody's company, except that of the beauties and the dancers. Look at Lord Trampleton, that enormous hulking monster, (who nevertheless dances beautifully, as all big men do), when he takes out his favourite partner, Miss Wirledge, to polk, his arm, as he whisks her round and round, forms radii of a circle of very considerable diameter. He almost wants a room to himself. Young men and women now, when they dance, dance really; it is no lazy sauntering, as of old, but downright hard work – after which they want air and refreshment. How can they get the one, when the rooms are filled with elderly folks; or the other, when we are squeezing round the supper tables, and drinking up all the available champagne and seltzer-water? No, no; the present plan, which I hear is becoming general, is admirable for London. Let there be half a dozen of good, active, bright-eyed chaperons and duennas, little women, who are more active, and keep a better lookout than your languishing voluptuous beauties' (I said this, casting at the same time a

look of peculiar tenderness towards Blanche Crowder); 'let
them keep watch and see that all is right – that the young men
don't dance too often with the same girl, or disappear on to the
balcony, and that sort of thing; let them have good large roomy
family coaches to carry the young women home to their
mammas. In a word, at a ball, let there be for the future no
admittance except upon business. In all the affairs of London
life, that is the rule, depend upon it.'

'And pray who told you, Mr Brown, that I didn't wish to
dance myself?' says Blanche, surveying her great person in the
looking glass (which could scarcely contain it) and flouncing out
of the room; and I actually believe that the unconscionable
creature, at her age and her size, is still thinking that she is a fairy,
and that the young fellows would like to dance round the room
with her. Ah, Bob! I remember that grotesque woman a slim
and graceful girl. I remember others tender and beautiful, whose
bright eyes glitter, and whose sweet voices whisper no more. So
they pass away – youth and beauty, love and innocence, pass
away and perish. I think of one now, whom I remember the
fairest and the gayest, the kindest and the purest; her laughter
was music – I can hear it still, though it will never echo anymore.
Far away, the silent tomb closes over her. Other roses than those
of our prime grow up and bloom, and have their day. Honest
youth, generous youth, may yours be as pure and as fair!

I did not think when I began to write it, that the last sentence
would have finished so; but life is not altogether jocular, Mr
Bob, and one comes upon serious thoughts suddenly as upon a
funeral in the street. Let us go back to the business we are upon,
namely, balls, whereof it, perhaps, has struck you that your
uncle has very little to say.

I saw one announced in the morning fashionable print
today, with a fine list of some of the greatest folks in London,
and had previously heard from various quarters how eager
many persons were to attend it, and how splendid an entertainment it was to be. And so the morning paper announced
that Mrs Hornby Madox threw open her house in So-and-so
Street, and was assisted in receiving her guests by Lady
Fugleman.

Now this is a sort of entertainment and arrangement than
which I confess I can conceive nothing more queer, though I

believe it is by no means uncommon in English society. Mrs
Hornby Madox comes into her fortune of ten thousand a year
– wishes to be presented in the London world, having lived in
the country previously – spares no expense to make her house
and festival as handsome as may be, and gets Lady Fugleman
to ask the company for her – not the honest Hornbys, not the
family Madoxes, not the jolly old squires and friends and
relatives of her family, and from her county; but the London
dandies and the London society: whose names you see chronicled at every party, and who, being Lady Fugleman's friends,
are invited by her ladyship to Mrs Hornby's house.

What a strange notion of society does this give – of
friendship, of fashion, of what people will do to be in the
fashion! Poor Mrs Hornby comes into her fortune, and says to
her old friends and family, 'My good people, I am going to cut
every one of you. You were very well as long as we were in
the country, where I might have my natural likings and
affections. But, henceforth, I am going to let Lady Fugleman
choose my friends for me. I know nothing about you
anymore. I have no objection to you, but if you want to know
me you must ask Lady Fugleman: if she says yes, I shall be
delighted: if no, *Bon jour.*'

This strange business goes on daily in London. Honest
people do it, and think not the least harm. The proudest and
noblest do not think they demean themselves by crowding to
Mrs Goldcalf's parties, and strike quite openly a union
between her wealth and their titles, to determine as soon as the
former ceases. There is not the least hypocrisy about this at
any rate – the terms of the bargain are quite understood on
every hand.

But oh, Bob! see what an awful thing it is to confess, and
would not even hypocrisy be better than this daring cynicism,
this open heartlessness – Godlessness I had almost called it? Do
you mean to say, you great folks, that your object in society is
not love, is not friendship, is not family union and affection –
is not truth and kindness; – is not generous sympathy and
union of Christian (pardon me the word, but I can indicate my
meaning by no other) – of Christian men and women, parents
and children, – but that you assemble and meet together, not
caring or trying to care for one another, – without a pretext of

good will – with a daring selfishness openly avowed? I am sure
I wish Mrs Goldcalf or the other lady no harm, and have never
spoken to, or set eyes on either of them, and I do not mean to
say, Mr Robert, that you and I are a whit better than they are,
and doubt whether they have made the calculation for themselves of the consequences of what they are doing. But as sure
as two and two make four, a person giving up of his own
accord his natural friends and relatives, for the sake of the
fashion, seems to me to say, I acknowledge myself to be
heartless: I turn my back on my friends, I disown my relatives,
and I dishonour my father and mother.

A WORD ABOUT DINNERS

English Society, my beloved Bob, has this eminent advantage over all other – that is, if there be any society left in the wretched distracted old European continent – that it is above all others a dinner-giving society. A people like the Germans, that dines habitually, and with what vast appetite I need not say, at one o'clock in the afternoon – like the Italians, that spends its evenings in opera-boxes – like the French, that amuses itself of nights with *eau sucrée* and intrigue – cannot, believe me, understand Society rightly. I love and admire my nation for its good sense, its manliness, its friendliness, its morality in the main – and these, I take it, are all expressed in that noble institution, the dinner.

The dinner is the happy end of the Briton's day. We work harder than the other nations of the earth. We do more, we live more in our time, than Frenchmen or Germans. Every great man amongst us likes his dinner, and takes to it kindly. I could mention the most august names of poets, statesmen, philosophers, historians, judges, and divines, who are as great at the dinner-table as in the field, the closet, the senate, or the bench. Gibbon mentions that he wrote the first two volumes of his history whilst a placeman in

London, lodging in St James's, going to the House of Commons, to the Club, and to dinner every day. The man flourishes under that generous and robust regimen; the healthy energies of society are kept up by it; our friendly intercourse is maintained; our intellect ripens with the good cheer, and throws off surprising crops, like the fields about Edinburgh, under the influence of that admirable liquid, Claret. The best wines are sent to this country therefore; for no other deserves them as ours does.

I am a diner-out, and live in London. I protest, as I look back at the men and diners I have seen in the last week, my mind is filled with manly respect and pleasure. How good they have been! how admirable the entertainments! how worthy the men!

Let me, without divulging names, and with a cordial gratitude, mention a few of those whom I have met and who have all done their duty.

Sir, I have sat at table with a great, a world-renowned statesman. I watched him during the progress of the banquet – I am at liberty to say that he enjoyed it like a man.

On another day, it was a celebrated literary character. It was beautiful to see him at his dinner: cordial and generous, jovial and kindly, the great author enjoyed himself as the great statesman – may he long give us good books and good dinners!

Yet another day, and I sat opposite to a Right Reverend Bishop. My Lord, I was pleased to see good thing after good thing disappear before you; and think no man ever better became that rounded episcopal apron. How amiable he was; how kind! He put water into his wine. Let us respect the moderation of the Church.

An then the men learned in the law: how they dine! what hospitality, what splendour, what comfort, what wine! As we walked away very gently in the moonlight, only three days since, from the —'s, a friend of my youth and myself, we could hardly speak for gratitude: 'Dear sir,' we breathed fervently, 'ask us soon again.' One never has too much at those perfect banquets – no hideous headaches ensue, or horrid resolutions about adopting Revalenta Arabica for the future – but contentment with all the world light slumbering, joyful waking to grapple with the morrow's work. Ah, dear Bob, those lawyers have great merits. There is a dear old judge at whose family table if I could see you seated, my desire in life would be pretty nearly fulfilled. If you make yourself agreeable there, you will be in a fair way to get on in the world. But you are a youth still. Youths go to balls: men go to dinners.

Doctors, again, notoriously eat well; when my excellent friend Sangrado takes a bumper, and saying, with a shrug and a twinkle of his eye, '*Video meliora proboque, deteriora sequor*', tosses off the wine, I always ask the butler for a glass of that bottle.

The inferior clergy, likewise, dine very much and well. I don't know when I have been better entertained, as far as creature comforts go, than by men of very Low Church principles; and one of the very best repasts that ever I saw in my life was at Darlington, given by a Quaker.

Some of the best wine in London is given to his friends by a poet of my acquaintance. All artists are notoriously fond of dinners, and invite you, but not so profusely. Newspaper editors delight in dinners on Saturdays, and give them, thanks to the present position of Literature, very often and good. Dear Bob, I have seen the mahoganies of many men.

Every evening between seven and eight o'clock, I like to look at the men dressed for dinner, perambulating the western districts of our city. I like to see the smile on their countenances lighted up with an indescribable self-importance and good-humour; the askance glances which they cast at the little streetboys and foot passengers who eye their shiny boots; the dainty manner in which they trip over the pavement on those boots, eschewing the mud-pools and dirty crossings; the refreshing whiteness of their linen; the coaxing twiddle which they give to the ties of their white chokers – the caress of a fond parent to an innocent child.

I like walking myself. Those who go in cabs or broughams, I have remarked, have not the same radiant expression which the pedestrian exhibits. A man in his own brougham has anxieties about the stepping of his horse, or the squaring of the groom's elbows, or a doubt whether Jones's turnout is not better; or whether something is not wrong in the springs; or whether he shall have the brougham out if the night is rainy.

They always look tragical behind the glasses. A cab diner-out has commonly some cares, lest his sense of justice should be injured by the overcharge of the driver (these fellows are not uncommonly exorbitant in their demands upon gentlemen whom they set down at good houses); lest the smell of tobacco left by the last occupants of the vehicle (five medical students, let us say, who have chartered the vehicle, and smoked cheroots from the London University to the playhouse in the Haymarket) should infest the clothes of Tom Lavender who is going to Lady Rosemary's; lest straws should stick unobserved to the glutinous lustre of his boots – his shiny ones, and he should appear in Dives's drawing-room like a poet with a *tenui avenâ*, or like Mad Tom in the play. I hope, my dear Bob, if a straw should ever enter a drawing-room in the wake of your boot, you will not be much disturbed in mind. Hark ye, in confidence; I have seen —* in a hack-cab. There is no harm in employing one. There is no harm in anything natural, any more.

I cannot help here parenthetically relating a story which occurred in my own youth, in the year 1815, at the time when I first made my own *entrée* into society (for everything must have a beginning, Bob; and though we have been gentlemen long before the Conqueror, and have always consorted with gentlemen, yet we had not always attained that *haute volée* of fashion which has distinguished some of us subsequently); I recollect, I say, in 1815, when the Marquis of Sweetbread was good enough to ask me and the late Mr Ruffles to dinner, to meet Prince Schwartzenberg and the Hetman Platoff. Ruffles was a man a good deal about town in those days, and certainly in very good society.

I was myself a young one, and thought Ruffles was rather inclined to patronize me: which I did not like. 'I would have you to know, Mr Ruffles,' thought I, 'that, after all, a gentleman can but be a gentleman; that though we Browns have no handles to our names, we are quite as well-bred as some folks who possess those ornaments' – and in time I determined to give him a lesson. So when he called for me in

---

* Mr Brown's MS. here contains a name of such prodigious dignity out of the 'P–r–ge,' that we really do not dare to print it.

the hackney-coach at my lodgings in Swallow Street, and we had driven under the *porte-cochère* of Sweetbread House, where two tall and powdered domestics in the uniform of the Sweetbreads, viz. a spinach-coloured coat, with waistcoat and the vest of delicate yellow or melted-butter colour, opened the doors of the hall – what do you think, sir, I did? In the presence of these gentlemen, who were holding on at the door, I offered to toss up with Ruffles, heads or tails, who should pay for the coach; and then purposely had a dispute with the poor Jarvey about the fare. Ruffles's face of agony during this transaction I shall never forget. Sir, it was like the Laocoon. Drops of perspiration trembled on his pallid brow, and he flung towards me looks of imploring terror that would have melted an ogre. A better fellow than Ruffles never lived – he is dead long since, and I don't mind owning to this harmless little deceit.

A person of some note – a favourite Snob of mine – I am told, when he goes to dinner, adopts what he considers a happy artifice, and sends his cab away at the corner of the street; so that the gentleman in livery may not behold its number, or that the lord with whom he dines, and about whom he is always talking, may not be supposed to know that Mr Smith came in a hack-cab.

A man who is troubled with a shame like this, Bob, is unworthy of any dinner at all. Such a man must needs be a sneak and a humbug, anxious about the effect which he is to produce: uneasy in his mind: a donkey in a lion's skin: a small pretender – distracted by doubts and frantic terrors of what is to come next. Such a man can be no more at ease in his chair at dinner than a man is in the fauteuil at the dentist's (unless indeed he go to the admirable Mr Gilbert in Suffolk Street, who is dragged into this essay for the benefit of mankind alone, and who, I vow, removes a grinder with so little pain, that all the world should be made aware of him) – a fellow, I say, ashamed of the original from which he sprung, of the cab in which he drives, awkward, therefore affected and un-natural, can never hope or deserve to succeed in society.

The great comfort of the society of great folks is, that they do not trouble themselves about your twopenny little person, as smaller persons do, but take you for what you are – a man kindly and good-natured, or witty and sarcastic, or learned and eloquent, or a good *raconteur*, or a very handsome man, (and in '15 some of the Browns were – but I am speaking of five-and-thirty years ago), or an excellent gourmand and judge of wines – or what not. Nobody sets you so quickly at your ease as a fine gentleman. I have seen more noise made about a knight's lady than about the Duchess of Fitzbattleaxe herself: and Lady Mountararat, whose family dates from the Deluge, enters and leaves a room, with her daughters, the lovely Ladies Eve and Lilith D'Arc, with much less pretension and in much simpler capotes and what-do-you-call-'ems, than Lady de Mogyns or Mrs Shindy, who quit an assembly in a whirlwind as it were, with trumpets and alarms like a stage king and queen.

But my pen can run no further, for my paper is out, and it is time to dress for dinner.

ON SOME OLD CUSTOMS OF THE DINNER-TABLE

f all the sciences which have made a progress in late years, I think, dear Bob (to return to the subject from which I parted with so much pleasure last week), that the art of dinner-giving has made the most delightful and rapid advances. Sir, I maintain, even now with a matured age and appetite, that the dinners of this present day are better than those we had in our youth, and I can't but be thankful at least once in every day for this decided improvement in our civilization. Those who remember the usages of five-and-twenty years back will be ready, I am sure, to acknowledge this progress. I was turning over at the Club yesterday a queer little book written at that period, which, I believe, had some authority at the time, and which records some of those customs which obtained, if not in good London society, at least in some companies, and parts of our islands. Sir, many of these practices seem as antiquated now as the usages described in the accounts of Homeric feasts, or Queen Elizabeth's banquets and breakfasts. Let us be happy to think they are gone.

The book in question is called 'The Maxims of Sir Morgan O'Doherty', a queer baronet, who appears to have lived in the first quarter of the century, and whose opinions the antiquarian may examine, not without profit – a strange barbarian indeed it is, and one wonders that such customs should ever have been prevalent in our country.

Fancy such opinions as these having ever been holden by any set of men among us. Maxim 2. – 'It is laid down in fashionable life that you must drink Champagne after white cheeses, water after red . . . Ale is to be avoided, in case a wet night is to be expected, as should cheese also.' Maxim 4. – 'A fine singer, after dinner, is to be avoided, for he is a great bore, and stops the wine . . . One of the best rules (to put him down) is to applaud him most vociferously as soon as he has sung the first verse, as if all was over, and say to the gentleman farthest from you at table that you admire the conclusion of this song very much.' Maxim 25. – 'You meet people occasionally who tell you it is bad taste to give Champagne at dinner – Port and Tenerife being such superior drinking,' &c. &c. I am copying out of a book printed three months since, describing ways prevalent when you were born. Can it be possible, I say, that England was ever in such a state?

Was it ever a maxim in 'fashionable life' that you were to drink champagne after white cheeses? What was that maxim in fashionable life about drinking and about cheese? The maxim in fashionable life is to drink what you will. It is too simple now to trouble itself about wine or about cheese. Ale again is to be avoided, this strange Doherty says, if you expect a wet night – and in another place he says 'the English drink a pint of porter at a draught.' – What English? gracious powers! Are we a nation of coalheavers? Do we ever have a wet night? Do we ever meet people occasionally who say that to give Champagne at dinner is bad taste, and that Port and Tenerife are such superior drinking? Fancy Tenerife, my dear boy – I say fancy a man asking you to drink Tenerife at dinner; the mind shudders at it – he might as well invite you to swallow the Peak.

And then consider the maxim about the fine singer who is to be avoided. What! was there a time in most people's memory, when folks at dessert began to sing? I have heard such a thing at a tenants' dinner in the country; but the idea of a fellow beginning to perform a song at a dinner-party in London fills my mind with terror and amazement; and I picture to myself any table which I frequent, in Mayfair, in Bloomsbury, in Belgravia, or where you will, and the pain which would seize upon the host and the company if some wretch were to commence a song.

We have passed that savage period of life. We do not want to hear songs from guests, we have the songs done for us; as we don't want our ladies to go down into the kitchen and cook the dinner any more. The cook can do it better and cheaper. We do not desire feats of musical or culinary skill – but simple, quiet, easy, unpretending conversation.

In like manner, there was a practice once usual, and which still lingers here and there, of making complimentary speeches after dinner; that custom is happily almost entirely discontinued. Gentlemen do not meet to compliment each other profusely, or to make fine phrases. Simplicity gains upon us daily. Let us be thankful that the florid style is disappearing.

I once shared a bottle of sherry with a commercial traveller at Margate who gave a toast or a sentiment as he filled every glass. He would not take his wine without this queer ceremony before it. I recollect one of his sentiments, which was as follows: 'Year is to 'er that doubles our joys, and divides our sorrows – I give you woman, sir,' – and we both emptied our glasses. These lumbering ceremonials are passing out of our manners, and were found only to obstruct our free intercourse. People can like each other just as much without orations, and be just as merry without being forced to drink against their will.

And yet there are certain customs to which one clings still; for instance, the practice of drinking wine with your neighbour, though wisely not so frequently indulged in as of old, yet still obtains, and I trust will never be abolished. For though, in the old time, when Mr and Mrs Fogy had sixteen friends to dinner, it became an unsupportable *corvée* for Mr F to ask sixteen persons to drink wine, and a painful task for Mrs Fogy to be called upon to bow to ten gentlemen, who desired to have the honour to drink her health, yet, employed in moderation, tha ancient custom of challenging your friends to drink is a kindly and hearty old usage, and productive of many most beneficial results.

I have known a man of a modest and reserved turn, (just like your old uncle, dear Bob, as no doubt you were going to remark), when asked to drink by the host, suddenly lighten up, toss off his glass, get confidence, and begin to talk right and left. He wanted but the spur to set him going. It is supplied by the butler at the back of his chair.

It sometimes happens, again, that a host's conversational powers are not brilliant. I own that I could point out a few such whom I have the honour to name among my friends – gentlemen, in fact, who wisely hold their tongues because they have nothing to say which is worth the hearing or the telling, and properly confine themselves to the carving of the mutton and the ordering of the wines. Such men, manifestly, should always be allowed, nay encouraged, to ask their guests to take wine. In putting that question, they show their goodwill, and cannot possibly betray their mental deficiency. For example, let us suppose Jones, who has been perfectly silent all dinner-time, oppressed, doubtless, by that awful Lady Tiara, who sits swelling on his right hand, suddenly rallies, singles me out, and with a loud cheering voice cries, 'Brown my boy, a glass of wine.' I reply, 'With pleasure, my dear Jones.' He responds as quick as thought, 'Shall it be hock or champagne, Brown?' I mention the wine which I prefer. He calls to the butler, and says, 'Some champagne or hock' (as the case may be, for I don't choose to commit myself) – 'some champagne or hock to Mr Brown'; and finally he says, 'Good health!' in a pleasant tone. Thus you see, Jones, though not a conversationist, has had the opportunity of making no less than four observations, which, if not brilliant or witty, are yet manly, sensible, and agreeable. And I defy any man in the metropolis, be he the most accomplished, the most learned, the wisest, or the most eloquent, to say more than Jones upon a similar occasion.

If you have had a difference with a man, and are desirous to make it up, how pleasant it is to take wine with him. Nothing is said but that simple phrase which has just been uttered by my friend Jones; and yet it means a great deal. The cup is a symbol of reconciliation. The other party drinks up your goodwill as you accept his token of returning friendship – and thus the liquor is hallowed which Jones has paid for: and I like to think that the grape which grew by Rhine or Rhone was born and ripened under the sun there, so as to be the means of bringing two good fellows together. I once heard the head physician of a Hydropathic establishment on the sunny banks of the first-named river, give the health of His Majesty the King of Prussia, and, calling upon the company to receive that august toast with a 'donnerndes Lebehoch', toss off a bumper of sparkling water. It did not seem to me a genuine enthusiasm. No, no, let us have toast and wine, not toast and water. It was not in vain that grapes grew on the hills of Father Rhine.

One seldom asks ladies now to take wine – except when, in a confidential whisper to the charming creature whom you have brought down to dinner, you humbly ask permission to pledge her, and she delicately touches her glass, with a fascinating smile, in reply to your glance, – a smile, you rogue, which goes to your heart. I say, one does not ask ladies anymore to take wine: and I think, this custom being abolished, the contrary practice should be introduced, and that the ladies should ask the gentlemen. I know one who did, *une grande dame de par le monde*, as honest Brantôme phrases it, and from whom I deserved no such kindness; but, sir, the effect of that graceful act of hospitality was such, that she made a grateful slave for ever of one who was an admiring rebel previously, who would do anything to show his gratitude, and who now knows no greater delight than when he receives a card which bears her respected name.*

A dinner of men is well now and again, but few well-regulated minds relish a dinner without women. There are some wretches who, I believe, still meet together for the sake of what is called 'the spread', who dine each other round and round, and have horrid delights in turtle, early peas, and other culinary luxuries – but I pity the condition as I avoid the

---

* Upon my word, Mr BROWN, this is too broad a hint. – *Punch*.

banquets of those men. The only substitute for ladies at dinners, or consolation for want of them, is – smoking. Cigars, introduced with the coffee, do, if anything can, make us forget the absence of the other sex. But what a substitute is that for her who doubles our joys, and divides our griefs! for woman! as my friend the Traveller said.

GREAT AND LITTLE DINNERS

It has been said, dear Bob, that I have seen the mahoganies of many men, and it is with no small feeling of pride and gratitude that I am enabled to declare also, that I hardly remember in my life to have had a bad dinner. Would to heaven that all mortal men could say likewise! Indeed, and in the presence of so much want and misery as pass under our ken daily, it is with a feeling of something like shame and humiliation that I make the avowal; but I have robbed no man of his meal that I know of, and am here speaking of very humble as well as very grand banquets, the which I maintain are, when there is a sufficiency, almost always good.

Yes, all dinners are good, from a shilling upwards. The plate of boiled beef which Mary, the neat-handed waitress, brings or used to bring you in the Old Bailey – I say used, for, ah me! I speak of years long past, when the cheeks of Mary were as blooming as the carrots which she brought up with the beef, and she may be a grandmother by this time, or a pallid ghost, far out of the regions of beef; – from the shilling dinner of beef and carrots to the grandest banquets of the season – everything is good. There are no degrees in eating. I mean that mutton is as good as venison – beefsteak, if you are hungry, as good as turtle – bottled ale, if you like it, to the full as good as champagne; – there is no delicacy in the world which Monsieur Francatelli or Monsieur Soyer can produce, which I believe to be better than toasted cheese. I have seen a dozen of epicures at a grand table forsake every French and Italian delicacy for boiled leg of pork and pease pudding. You can but be hungry, and eat and be happy.

What is the moral I would deduce from this truth, if truth it be? I would have a great deal more hospitality practised than is common among us – more hospitality and less show. Properly considered, the quality of dinner is twice blest; it blesses him that gives, and him that takes: a dinner with friendliness is the best of all friendly meetings – a pompous entertainment, where no love is, the least satisfactory.

Why, then, do we of the middle classes persist in giving entertainments so costly, and beyond our means? This will be read by many mortals, who are aware that they live on leg of mutton themselves, or worse than this, have what are called meat teas, than which I cannot conceive a more odious custom; that ordinarily they are very sober in their way of life; that they like in reality that leg of mutton better than the condiments of that doubtful French artist who comes from the pastrycook's, and presides over the mysterious stewpans in the kitchen; why, then, on their company dinners, should they flare up in the magnificent manner in which they universally do?

Everybody has the same dinner in London, and the same soup, saddle of mutton, boiled fowls and tongue, *entrées*, champagne, and so forth. I own myself to being no better nor worse than my neighbours in this respect, and rush off to the confectioners' for sweets, &c; hire sham butlers and attendants; have a fellow going round the table with still and dry champagne, as if I knew his name, and it was my custom to drink those wines every day of my life. I am as bad as my neighbours: but why are we so bad, I ask? – why are we not more reasonable?

If we receive very great men or ladies at our houses, I will lay a wager that they will select mutton and gooseberry tart for their dinner: forsaking the *entrées* which the men in white Berlin gloves are handing round in the Birmingham plated dishes. Asking lords and ladies, who have great establishments of their own, to French dinners and delicacies, is like inviting a grocer to a meal of figs, or a pastrycook to a banquet of raspberry tarts. They have had enough of them. And great folks, if they like you, take no count of your feasts, and grand preparations, and can but eat mutton like men.

One cannot have sumptuary laws nowadays, or restrict the gastronomical more than any other trade: but I wish a check could be put upon our dinner extravagances by some means, and am confident that the pleasures of life would greatly be increased by moderation. A man might give two dinners for one, according to the present pattern. Half your money is swallowed up in a dessert, which nobody wants in the least, and which I always grudge to see arriving at the end of plenty. Services of culinary kickshaws swallow up money, and give nobody pleasure, except the pastrycook, whom they enrich. Everybody entertains as if he had three or four thousand a year.

Someone with a voice potential should cry out against this overwhelming luxury. What is mere decency in a very wealthy man is absurdity – nay, wickedness in a poor one: a frog by nature, I am an insane, silly creature, to attempt to swell myself to the size of the ox, my neighbour. Oh, that I could establish in the middle classes of London an Anti-entrée and Anti-Dessert movement! I would go down to posterity not ill-deserving of my country in such a case, and might be ranked among the social benefactors. Let us have a meeting at Willis's Rooms, Ladies and Gentlemen, for the purpose, and get a few philanthropists, philosophers, and bishops or so, to speak! As people, in former days, refused to take sugar, let us get up a society which shall decline to eat dessert and made dishes. *

In this way, I say, every man who now gives a dinner might give two; and take in a host of poor friends and relatives, who are now excluded from his hospitality. For dinners are given mostly in the middle classes by way of revenge; and Mr and Mrs Thompson ask Mr and Mrs Johnson, because the latter

* Mr Brown here enumerates three *entrées*, which he confesses he can *not* resist, and likewise preserved cherries at dessert: but the principle is good, though the man is weak.

have asked them. A man at this rate who gives fours dinners of twenty persons in the course of the season, each dinner costing him something very near upon thirty pounds, receives in return, we will say, forty dinners from the friends whom he has himself invited. That is, Mr and Mrs Johnson pay a hundred and twenty pounds, as do all their friends, for forty-four dinners of which they partake. So that they may calculate that everytime they dine with their respective friends, they pay about twenty-eight shillings per *tête*. What a sum this is, dear Johnson, for you and me to spend upon our waistcoats! What does poor Mrs Johnson care for all these garish splendours, who has had her dinner at two with her dear children in the nursery? Our custom is not hospitality or pleasure, but to be able to cut off a certain number of acquaintance from the dining list.

One of these dinners of twenty, again, is scarcely ever pleasant as far as regards society. You may chance to get near a pleasant neighbour and neighbouress, when your corner of the table is possibly comfortable. But there can be no general conversation. Twenty people cannot engage together in talk. You would want a speaking-trumpet to communicate from your place by the lady of the house (for I wish to give my respected reader the place of honour) to the lady at the opposite corner at the right of the host. If you have a joke or a *mot* to make, you cannot utter it before such a crowd. A joke is nothing which can only get a laugh out of a third part of the company. The most eminent wags of my acquaintance are dumb in these great parties; and your *raconteur* or story-teller, if he is prudent, will invariably hold his tongue. For what can be more odious than to be compelled to tell a story at the top of your voice, to be called on to repeat it for the benefit of a distant person who has only heard a part of the anecdote? There are stories of mine which would fail utterly, were they narrated in any but an undertone; others in which I laugh, am overcome by emotion, and so forth – what I call my *intimes* stories. Now it is impossible to do justice to these except in the midst of a general hush, and in a small circle; so that I am commonly silent. And as no anecdote is positively new in a party of twenty, the chances are so much against you that somebody should have heard the story before, in which case you are done.

In these large assemblies, a wit, then, is of no use, and does not have a chance: a *raconteur* does not get a fair hearing, and both of these real ornaments of a dinner-table are thus utterly thrown away. I have seen Jack Jolliffe, who can keep a table of eight or ten persons in a roar of laughter for four hours, remain utterly mute in a great entertainment, smothered by the numbers and the Dowager on each side of him: and Tom Yarnold, the most eminent of conversationists, sit through a dinner as dumb as the footman behind him. They do not care to joke, unless there is a sympathizing society, and prefer to be silent rather than throw their good things away.

What I would recommend, then, with all my power, is, that dinners should be more simple, more frequent, and should comprise fewer persons. Ten is the utmost number that a man of moderate means should ever invite to his table; although in a great house, managed by a great establishment, the case may be different. A man and woman may look as if they were glad to see ten people: but in a great dinner they abdicate their position as host and hostess, – are mere creatures in the hands of the sham butlers, sham footmen, and tall confectioners' emissaries who crowd the room, – and are guests at their own table, where they are helped last, and of which they occupy the top and bottom. I have marked many a lady watching with timid glances the large artificial *major-domo*, who officiates for that night only, and thought to myself, 'Ah, my dear madam, how much happier might we all be if there were but half the splendour, half the made dishes, and half the company assembled.'

If any dinner-giving person who reads this shall be induced by my representations to pause in his present career, to cut off some of the luxuries of his table, and instead of giving one enormous feast to twenty persons to have three simple dinners for ten, my dear Nephew will not have been addressed in vain. Everybody will be bettered; and while the guests will be better pleased, and more numerous, the host will actually be left with money in his pocket.

ON LOVE, MARRIAGE, MEN, AND WOMEN

I

ob Brown is in love, then, and undergoing the common lot! And so, my dear lad, you are this moment enduring the delights and tortures, the jealousy and wakefulness, the longing and raptures, the frantic despair and elation, attendant upon the passion of love. In the year 1812, (it was before I contracted my alliance with your poor dear Aunt, who never caused me any of the disquietudes above enumerated), I myself went through some of those miseries and pleasures which you now, O my Nephew, are enduring. I pity and sympathize with you. I am an old cock now, with a feeble strut and a faltering crow. But I was young once: and remember the time very well. Since that time, *amavi amantes*: if I see two young people happy, I like it, as I like to see children enjoying a pantomime. I have been the confidant of numbers of honest fellows, and the secret watcher of scores of little pretty intrigues in life. Miss Y, I know why you go so eagerly to balls now, and Mr Z, what has set you off dancing at your mature age. Do you fancy, Mrs Alpha, that I believe you walk every day at half past eleven by the Serpentine for nothing, and that I don't see young O'Mega in Rotten Row? . . . And so, my poor Bob, you are shot.

If you lose the object of your desires, the loss won't kill you; you may set that down as a certainty. If you win, it is possible that you will be disappointed; that point also is to be considered. But hit or miss, good luck or bad – I should be sorry, my honest Bob, that thou didst not undergo the malady. Every man ought to be in love a few times in his life, and to have a smart attack of the fever. You are the better for it when it is over: the better for your misfortune if you endure it with a manly heart; how much the better for success if you win it and a good wife into the bargain! Ah! Bob – there is a stone in the burying ground at Funchal which I often and often think of – many hopes and passions lie beneath it, along with the fairest and gentlest creature in the world – it's not Mrs Brown that lies there. After life's fitful fever, she sleeps in Marylebone burying ground, poor dear soul! Emily Blenkinsop *might* have been Mrs Brown, but – but let us change the subject.

Of course you will take advice, my dear Bob, about your flame. All men and women do. It is notorious that they listen to the opinions of all their friends, and never follow their own counsel. Well, tell us about this girl. What are her qualifications, expectations, belongings, station in life, and so forth?

About beauty I do not argue. I take it for granted. A man sees beauty, or that which he likes, with eyes entirely his own. I don't say that plain women get husbands as readily as the pretty girls – but so many handsome girls are unmarried, and so many of the other sort wedded, that there is no possibility of establishing a rule, or of setting up a standard. Poor dear Mrs Brown was a far finer woman than Emily Blenkinsop, and yet I loved Emily's little finger more than the whole hand which your Aunt Martha gave me – I see the plainest women exercising the greatest fascinations over men – in fine, a man falls in love with a woman because it is fate, because she is a woman; Bob, too, is a man, and endowed with a heart and a beard.

Is she a clever woman? I do not mean to disparage you, my

good fellow, but you are not a man that is likely to set the Thames on fire; and I should rather like to see you fall to the lot of a clever woman. A set has been made against clever women in all times. Take all Shakespeare's heroines – they all seem to me pretty much the same – affectionate, motherly, tender, that sort of thing. Take Scott's ladies, and other writers' – each man seems to draw from one model – an exquisite slave is what we want for the most part; a humble, flattering, smiling, child-loving, tea-making, pianoforte-playing being, who laughs at our jokes, however old they may be, coaxes and wheedles us in our humours, and fondly lies to us through life. I never could get your poor Aunt into this system, though I confess I should have been a happier man had she tried it.

There are many more clever women in the world than men think for. Our habit is to despise them; we believe they do not think because they do not contradict us; and are weak because they do not struggle and rise up against us. A man only begins to know women as he grows old; and for my part my opinion of their cleverness rises everyday.

When I say I know women, I mean I know that I don't know them. Every single woman I ever knew is a puzzle to me, as I have no doubt she is to herself. Say they are not clever? Their hypocrisy is a perpetual marvel to me, and a constant exercise of cleverness of the finest sort. You see a demure-looking woman perfect in all her duties, constant in house-bills and shirt buttons, obedient to her lord, and anxious to please him in all things; silent when you and he talk politics, or literature, or balderdash together, and if referred to, saying, with a smile of perfect humility, 'Oh, women are not judges upon such and such matters; we leave learning and politics to men.' 'Yes, poor Polly,' says Jones, patting the back of Mrs J's head good-naturedly, 'attend to the house, my dear; that's the best thing you can do, and leave the rest to us.' Benighted idiot! She has long ago taken your measure and your friends'; she knows your weaknesses, and ministers to them in a thousand artful ways. She knows your obstinate points, and marches round them with the most curious art and patience, as you will see an ant on a journey turn round an obstacle. Every woman manages her husband: every person who manages another is a hypocrite. Her smiles, her submission, her good-humour, for all which we value her, – what are they but admirable duplicity? We expect falseness from her, and order and educate her to be dishonest. Should he upbraid, I'll own that he prevail; say that he frown, I'll answer with a smile; – what are these but lies, that we exact from our slaves? – lies, the dexterous performance of which we announce to be the female virtues; brutal Turks that we are! I do not say that Mrs Brown ever obeyed me – on the contrary: but I should have liked it, for I am a Turk like my neighbour.

I will instance your mother now. When my brother comes in to dinner after a bad day's sport, or after looking over the bills of some of you boys, he naturally begins to be surly with your poor dear mother, and to growl at the mutton. What does she do? She may be hurt, but she doesn't show it. She proceeds to coax, to smile, to turn the conversation, to stroke down Bruin, and get him in a good humour. She sets him on his old stories, and she and all the girls – poor dear little Sapphiras! – set off laughing; there is that story about the Goose walking into church, which your father tells, and your mother and sisters laugh at, until I protest I am so ashamed that I hardly know where to look. On he goes with that story time after time: and your poor mother sits there and knows that I know she is a humbug, and laughs on; and teaches all the girls to laugh too. Had that dear creature been born to wear a nose-ring and bangles instead of a muff and bonnet; and had she a brown skin in the place of that fair one with which Nature has endowed her, she would have done Suttee, after your brown Brahmin father had died, and thought women very irreligious too, who refused to roast themselves for their masters and lords. I do not mean to say that the late Mrs Brown would have gone through the process of incremation for me – far from it: by a timely removal she was spared from the grief which her widowhood would have doubtless caused her, and I acquiesce in the decrees of Fate in this instance, and have not the least desire to have preceded her.

I hope the ladies will not take my remarks in ill part. If I die for it, I must own that I don't think they have fair play. In the bargain we make with them I don't think they get their rights. And as a labourer notoriously does more by the piece than he does by the day, and a free man works harder than a slave, so I doubt whether we get the most out of our women by enslaving them as we do by law and custom. There are some folks who would limit the range of women's duties to little more than a kitchen range – others who like them to administer to our delectation in a ballroom, and permit them to display dimpled shoulders and flowing ringlets – just as you have one horse for a mill, and another for the Park. But in whatever way we like them, it is for our use somehow that we have women brought up; to work for us, or to shine for us, or to dance for us, or what not? It would not have been thought shame of our fathers fifty years ago, that they could not make a custard or a pie, but our mothers would have been rebuked had they been ignorant on these matters. Why should not you and I be ashamed now because we cannot make our own shoes, or cut out our own breeches? We know better: we can get cobblers and tailors to do that – and it was we who made the laws for women, who, we are in the habit of saying, are not so clever as we are.

My dear Nephew, as I grow old and consider these things, I know which are the stronger, men or women; but which are the cleverer, I doubt.

ON LOVE, MARRIAGE, MEN, AND WOMEN

II

ong years ago, indeed it was at the Peace of Amiens, when with several other young bucks I was making the grand tour, I recollect how sweet we all of us were upon the lovely Duchess of Montepulciano at Naples, who, to be sure, was not niggardly of her smiles in return. There came a man amongst us, however, from London, a very handsome young fellow, with such an air of fascinating melancholy in his looks, that he cut out all the other suitors of the Duchess in the course of a week, and would have married her very likely, but that war was declared while this youth was still hankering about his Princess, and he was sent off to Verdun, whence he did not emerge for twelve years, and until he was as fat as a porpoise, and the Duchess was long since married to General Count Raff, one of the Emperor's heroes.

I mention poor Tibbits to show the curious difference of manner which exists among us; and which, though not visible to foreigners, is instantly understood by English people. Brave, clever, tall, slim, dark, and sentimental-looking, he passed muster in a foreign saloon, and as I must own to you, cut us fellows out: whereas we English knew instantly that the man was not well bred, by a thousand little signs, not to be understood by the foreigner. In his early youth, for instance, he had been cruelly deprived of his *h*'s by his parents, and though he tried to replace them in after life, they were no more natural than a glass eye, but stared at you as it were in a ghastly manner out of the conversation, and pained you by their horrid intrusions. Not acquainted with these refinements of our language, foreigners did not understand what Tibbits' errors were, and doubtless thought it was from envy that we conspired to slight the poor fellow.

I mention Mr Tibbits, because he was handsome, clever, honest, and brave, and in almost all respects our superior; and yet laboured under disadvantages of manner which unfitted him for certain society. It is not Tibbits the man, it is not Tibbits the citizen, of whom I would wish to speak lightly; his morals, his reading, his courage, his generosity, his talents are undoubted – it is the social Tibbits of whom I speak: and as I do not go to balls, because I do not dance, or to meetings of the Political Economy Club, or other learned associations, because taste and education have not fitted me for the pursuits for which other persons are adapted, so Tibbits' sphere is not in drawing-rooms, where the *h*, and other points of etiquette, are rigorously maintained.

I say thus much because one or two people have taken some remarks of mine in ill part, and hinted that I am a Tory in disguise: and an aristocrat that should be hung up to a lamp post. Not so, dear Bob; – there is nothing like the truth, about whomsoever it may be. I mean no more disrespect towards any fellow man by saying that he is not what is called in Society well bred, than by stating that he is not tall or short, or that he cannot dance, or that he does not know Hebrew, or whatever the case may be. I mean that if a man works with a pickaxe or shovel all day, his hands will be harder than those of a lady of fashion, and that his opinion about Madame Sontag's singing, or the last new novel, will not probably be of much value. And though I own my conviction that there are some animals which frisk advantageously in ladies' drawing-rooms, whilst others pull stoutly at the plough, I do not most certainly mean to reflect upon a horse for not being a lap-dog, or see that he has any cause to be ashamed that he is other than a horse.

And, in a word, as you are what is called a gentleman yourself, I hope that Mrs Bob Brown, whoever she may be, is not only by nature, but by education, a gentlewoman. No man ought ever to be called upon to blush for his wife. I see good men rush into marriage with ladies of whom they are afterwards ashamed; and in the same manner charming women linked to partners, whose vulgarity they try to screen. Poor Mrs Botibol, what a constant hypocrisy your life is, and how you insist upon informing everybody that Botibol is the best of men! Poor Jack Jinkins! what a female is that you brought back from Bagnigge Wells to introduce to London society! a handsome, tawdry, flaunting, watering-place belle; a boarding-house beauty: tremendous in brazen ornaments and cheap finery.

If you marry, dear Bob, I hope Mrs Robert B will be a lady not very much above or below your own station.

I would sooner that you should promote your wife, than that she should advance you. And though every man can point you out instances where his friends have been married to ladies of superior rank, who have accepted their new position with perfect grace, and made their husbands entirely happy; as there are examples of maid-servants decorating coronets, and semp-stresses presiding worthily over Baronial Halls; yet I hope Mrs Robert Brown will not come out of a palace or a kitchen: but of a house something like yours, out of a family something like yours, with a snug jointure something like that modest portion which I dare say you will inherit.

I remember when Arthur Rowdy (who I need not tell you belongs to the firm of Stumpy, Rowdy & Co., of Lombard Street, Bankers), married Lady Cleopatra; what a grand match it was thought by the Rowdy family; and how old Mrs Rowdy in Portman Square was elated at the idea of her son's new connection. Her daughters were to go to all the parties in London; and her house was to be filled with the very greatest of great folks. We heard of nothing but dear Lady Stonehenge from morning till night; and the old frequenters of the house were perfectly pestered with stories of dear Lady Zenobia and dear Lady Cornelia, and of the dear Marquis, whose masterly translation of *Cornelius Nepos* had placed him among the most learned of our nobility.

When Rowdy went to live in Mayfair, what a wretched house it was into which he introduced such of his friends as were thought worthy of presentation to his new society! The rooms were filled with young dandies of the Stonehenge connection – beardless bucks from Downing Street, gay young sprigs of the Guards – their sisters and mothers, their kith and kin. They overdrew their accounts at Rowdy's Bank, and laughed at him in his drawing-room; they made their bets and talked their dandy talk over his claret, at which the poor fellow sat quite silent. Lady Stonehenge invaded his nursery, appointed and cashiered his governess and children's maids; established her apothecary in permanence over him: quarrelled with old Mrs Rowdy, so that the poor old body was only allowed to see her grandchildren by stealth, and have secret interviews with them in the garden of Berkeley Square; made Rowdy take villas at Tunbridge, which she filled with her own family; massacred her daughter's visiting-book, in the which Lady Cleopatra, a good-natured woman, at first admitted some of her husband's relatives and acquaintance; and carried him abroad upon excursions, in which all he had to do was to settle the bills with the courier. And she went so far as to order him to change his side of the House and his politics, and adopt those of Lord Stonehenge, which were of the age of the Druids, his lordship's ancestors; but here the honest British merchant made a stand and conquered his mother-in-law, who would have smothered him the other day for voting for Rothschild. If it were not for the Counting House in the morning and the House of Commons at night, what would become of Rowdy? They say he smokes there, and drinks when he smokes. He has been known to go to Vauxhall, and has even been seen, with a comforter over his nose, listening to *Sam Hall* at the Cider Cellars. All this misery and misfortune came to the poor fellow for marrying out of his degree. The clerks at Lombard Street laugh when Lord Mistletoe steps out of his cab and walks into the bank parlour; and Rowdy's private account invariably tells tales of the visit of his young scapegrace of a brother-in-law.

Let us now, beloved and ingenuous youth, take the other side of the question, and discourse a little while upon the state of that man who takes unto himself a wife inferior to him in degree. I have before me in my acquaintance many most pitiable instances of individuals who have made this fatal mistake.

Although old fellows are as likely to be made fools as young in love matters, and Dan Cupid has no respect for the most venerable age, yet I remark that it is generally the young men who marry vulgar wives. They are on a reading tour for the Long Vacation, they are quartered at Ballinafad, they see Miss Smith or Miss O'Shaughnessy every day, healthy, lively, jolly girls with red cheeks, bright eyes, and high spirits – they come away at the end of the vacation, or when the regiment changes its quarters engaged men, family rows ensue, mothers cry out, papas grumble, Miss pines and loses her health at Baymouth or Ballinafad – consent is got at last, Jones takes his degree, Jenkins gets his company; Miss Smith and Miss O'Shaughnessy become Mrs Jones and Mrs Jenkins.

For the first year it is all very well. Mrs Jones is a great bouncing handsome creature, lavishly fond of her adored Jones, and caring for no other company but his. They have a cottage at Bayswater. He walks her out every evening. He sits and reads the last new novel to her whilst she works slippers for him, or makes some little tiny caps, and – dear Julia, dear Edward! – they are all in all to one another.

Old Mrs Smith of course comes up from Swansea at the time when the little caps are put into requisition, and takes possession of the cottage at Bayswater. Mrs Jones Senior calls upon Mrs Edward Jones's mamma, and, of course, is desirous to do everything that is civil to the family of Edward's wife.

Mrs Jones finds in the mother-in-law of her Edward a large woman with a cotton umbrella, who dines in the middle of the day, and has her beer, and who calls Mrs Jones Mum. What a state they are in in Pocklington Square about this woman! How can they be civil to her? Whom can they ask to meet her! How the girls, Edward's sisters, go on about her! Fanny says she ought to be shown to the housekeeper's room when she calls; Mary proposes that Mrs Shay, the washerwoman, should be invited on the day when Mrs Smith comes to dinner; and Emma (who was Edward's favourite sister, and who considers herself jilted by his marriage with Julia), points out the most dreadful thing of all, that Mrs Smith and Julia are exactly alike, and that in a few years Mrs Edward Jones will be the very image of that great enormous unwieldy horrid old woman.

Closeted with her daughter, of whom and of her baby she has taken possession, Mrs Smith gives her opinion about the Joneses: – They may be very good, but they are too fine ladies for *her*; and they evidently think she is not good enough for *them*: they are sad worldly people, and have never sat under a good minister, that is clear: they talked French before her on the day she called in Pocklington Gardens, 'and though they were laughing at me, I'm sure I can pardon them,' Mrs Smith says. Edward and Julia have a little altercation about the manner in which his family has treated Mrs Smith, and Julia, bursting into tears as she clasps her child to her bosom, says, 'My child, my child, will you be taught to be ashamed of your mother?'

Edward flings out of the room in a rage. It is true that Mrs Smith is not fit to associate with his family, and that her manners are not like theirs; that Julia's eldest brother, who is a serious tanner at Cardiff, is not a pleasant companion after dinner: and that it is not agreeable to be called 'Ned' and 'Old Cove' by her younger brother, who is an attorney's clerk in Gray's Inn, and favours Ned by asking him to lend him a 'Sov.', and by coming to dinner on Sundays. It is true that the appearance of that youth at the first little party the Edward Joneses gave after their marriage, when Natty disgracefully inebriated himself, caused no little scandal amongst his friends, and much wrath on the part of old Jones, who said, 'That little scamp calls my daughters by their Christian names! – a little beggar that is not fit to sit down in my hall. If ever he dares to call at my house I'll tell Jobbins to fling a pail of water over him.' And it is true that Natty called many times in Pocklington Square, and complained to Edward that he, Nat, could neither see his Mar nor the Gurls, and that the old gent cut up uncommon stiff.

So you see Edward Jones has had his way, and got a handsome wife, but at what expense? He and his family are separated. His wife brought him nothing but good looks. Her stock of brains is small. She is not easy in the new society into which she has been brought, and sits quite mum both at the grand parties which the old Joneses give in Pocklington Square, and at the snug little entertainments which poor Edward Jones tries on his own part. The women of the Jones' set try her in every way, and can get no good from her: Jones's male friends, who are civilized beings, talk to her, and receive only monosyllables in reply. His house is a stupid one; his acquaintances drop off; he has no circle at all at last, except, to be sure, that increasing family circle which brings up old Mrs Smith from Swansea every year.

What is the lot of a man at the end of a dozen years who has a wife like this? She is handsome no longer, and she never had any other merit. He can't read novels to her all through his life, while she is working slippers – it is absurd. He can't be philandering in Kensington Gardens with a lady who does not walk out now except with two nursemaids and the twins in a go-cart. He is a young man still, when she is an old woman. Love is a mighty fine thing, dear Bob, but it is not the life of a man. There are a thousand other things for him to think of besides the red lips of Lucy, or the bright eyes of Eliza. There is business, there is friendship, there is society, there are taxes, there is ambition, and the manly desire to exercise the talents which are given us by heaven, and reap the prize of our desert. There are other books in a man's library besides Ovid; and after dawdling ever so long at a woman's knee, one day he gets up and is free. We have all been there: we have all had the fever: the strongest and the smallest, from Samson, Hercules, Rinaldo, downwards; but it burns out, and you get well.

Ladies who read this, and who know what a love I have for the whole sex, will not, I hope, cry out at the above observations, or be angry because I state that the ardour of love declines after a certain period. My dear Mrs Hopkins, you would not have Hopkins to carry on the same absurd behaviour which he exhibited when he was courting you? or in place of going to bed and to sleep comfortably, sitting up half the night to write to you bad verses? You would not have him racked with jealousy if you danced or spoke with anyone else at a ball; or neglect all his friends, his business, his interest in life, in order to dangle at your feet? No, you are a sensible woman; you know that he must go to his counting-house, that he must receive and visit his friends, and that he must attend to his and your interest in life. You are no longer his goddess, his fairy, his peerless paragon, whose name he shouted as Don Quixote did that of Dulcinea. You are Jane Hopkins, you are thirty years old, you have got a parcel of children, and Hop loves you and them with all his heart. He would be a helpless driveller and ninny were he to be honeymooning still, whereas he is a good honest fellow, respected on 'Change, liked by his friends, and famous for his port-wine.

Yes, Bob, the fever goes, but the wife doesn't. Long after your passion is over, Mrs Brown will be at your side, good soul, still; and it is for that, as I trust, long subsequent period of my worthy Bob's life, that I am anxious. How will she look when the fairy brilliancy of the honeymoon has faded into the light of common day?

You are of a jovial and social turn, and like to see the world, as why should you not? It contains a great number of kind and honest folks, from whom you may hear a thousand things wise and pleasant. A man ought to like his neighbours, to mix with his neighbours, to be popular with his neighbours. It is a friendly heart that has plenty of friends. You can't be talking to Mrs Brown for ever and ever: you will be a couple of old geese if you do.

She ought then to be able to make your house pleasant to your friends. She ought to attract them to it by her grace, her good breeding, her good humour. Let it be said of her, 'What an uncommonly nice woman Mrs Brown is!' Let her be, if not a clever woman, an appreciator of cleverness in others, which, perhaps, clever folks like better. Above all, let her have a sense of humour, my dear Bob, for a woman without a laugh in her (like the late excellent Mrs Brown) is the greatest bore in existence. Life without laughing is a dreary blank. A woman who cannot laugh is a wet blanket on the kindly nuptial couch. A good laugh is sunshine in a house. A quick intelligence, a brightening eye, a kind smile, a cheerful spirit, – these, I hope, Mrs Bob will bring to you in her *trousseau*, to be used afterwards for daily wear. Before all things, my dear Nephew, try and have a cheerful wife.

What, indeed, does not that word 'cheerfulness' imply? It means a contented spirit, it means a pure heart, it means a kind and loving disposition; it means humility and charity; it means a generous appreciation of others, and a modest opinion of self. Stupid people, people who do not know how to laugh, are always pompous and self-conceited; that is, bigoted; that is, cruel; that is, ungentle, uncharitable, unchristian. Have a good, jolly, laughing, kind woman, then, for your partner, you who are yourself a kind and jolly fellow; and when you go to sleep, and when you wake, I pray there may be a smile under each of your honest nightcaps.

OUT OF TOWN

I

I have little news, my dear Bob, wherewith to entertain thee from this city, from which almost everybody has fled within the last week, and which lies in a state of torpor. I wonder what the newspapers find to talk about day after day, and how they come out every morning. But for a little distant noise of cannonading from the Danube and the Theiss, the whole world is silent, and London seems to have hauled down her flag, as her Majesty has done at Pimlico, and the Queen of cities has gone out of town.

You, in pursuit of Miss Kicklebury, are probably by this time at Spa or Homburg. Watch her well, Bob, and see what her temper is like. See whether she flirts with the foreigners much, examine how she looks of a morning (you will have a hundred opportunities of familiarity, and can drop in and out of a friend's apartments at a German watering-place as you never can hope to do here), examine her conduct with her little sisters, if they are of the party, whether she is good and playful with them, see whether she is cheerful and obedient to old Lady Kick (I acknowledge a hard task) – in fine, try her manners and temper, and see whether she wears them all day, or only puts on her smiles with her fresh bonnet, to come out on the parade at music time. I, meanwhile, remain behind, alone in our airy and great Babylon.

As an old soldier when he gets his ground begins straightway *à se caser*, as the French say, makes the most of his circumstances, and himself as comfortable as he can, an old London man, if obliged to pass the dull season in town, accommodates himself to the time, and forages here and there in the deserted city, and manages to make his own tent snug. A thousand means of comfort and amusement spring up, whereof a man has no idea of the existence, in the midst of the din and racket of the London season. I, for my part, am grown to that age, sir, when I like the quiet time the best: the gaiety of the great London season is too strong and noisy for me; I like to talk to my beloved metropolis when she has done dancing at crowded balls, and squeezing at concerts, and chattering at conversaziones, and gorging at great dinners – when she is calm, contemplative, confidential, and at leisure.

Colonel Padmore of our Club being out of town, and too wise a man to send his favourite old cob to grass, I mounted him yesterday, and took a ride in Rotten Row, and in various parts of the city, where but ten days back all sorts of life, hilarity, and hospitality, were going on. What a change it is now in the Park, from that scene which the modern Pepys, and that ingenious youth who signs his immortal drawings with a D surmounted by a dickey-bird, depicted only a few weeks ago! Where are the thousands of carriages that crawled along the Serpentine shore, and which give an observant man a happy and wholesome sense of his own insignificance – for you shall be a man long upon the town, and pass five hundred equipages without knowing the owners of one of them? Where are the myriads of horsemen who trampled the Row? – the splendid dandies whose boots were shiny, whose chins were tufted, whose shirts were astounding, whose manners were frank and manly, whose brains were somewhat small? Where are the stout old capitalists and bishops on their cobs (the Bench, by the way, cuts an uncommonly good figure on horseback)? Where are the dear rideresses, above all? Where is she the gleaming of whose red neck-ribbon in the distance made your venerable uncle's heart beat, Bob? He sees her now prancing by, severe and beautiful – a young Diana, with pure bright eyes! Where is Fanny, who wore the pretty grey hat and feather, and rode the pretty grey mare? Fanny changed her name last week, without ever so much as sending me a piece of cake. The gay squadrons have disappeared: the ground no longer thrills with the thump of their countless hoofs. Watteau-like groups in shot silks no longer compose themselves under the green boughs of Kensington Gardens: the scarlet trumpeters have blown themselves away thence; you don't behold a score of horsemen in the course of an hour's ride; and Mrs Catherine Highflyer, whom a fortnight since you never saw unaccompanied by some superb young Earl and *roué* of the fashion, had yesterday so little to do with her beautiful eyes, that she absolutely tried to kill your humble servant with them as she cantered by me in at the barriers of the Row, and looked round firing Parthian shots behind her. But Padmore's cob did not trot, nor did my blood run, any the quicker, Mr Bob; man and beast are grown too old and steady to be put out of our pace by any Mrs Highflyer of them all; and though I hope, if I live to be a hundred, never to be unmoved by the sight of a pretty girl, it is not thy kind of beauty, O ogling and vain Delilah, that can set me cantering after thee.

By the way, one of the benefits I find in the dull season is at my own lodgings. When I ring the bell now, that uncommonly pretty young woman, the landlady's daughter, condescends to come in and superintend my comfort, and whisk about amongst the books and tea-things, and wait upon me in general: whereas in the full season, when young Lord Claude Lollypop is here attending to his arduous duties in Parliament, and occupying his accustomed lodgings on the second floor, the deuce a bit will Miss Flora ever deign to bring a message or a letter to old Mr Brown on the first, but sends me in Muggins, my old servant, whose ugly face I have known any time these thirty years, or the blowsy maid-of-all-work with her sandy hair in papers.

Again, at the Club, how many privileges does a man lingering in London enjoy, from which he is precluded in the full season? Every man in every Club has three or four special aversions – men who somehow annoy him, as I have no doubt but that you and I, Bob, are hated by some particular man, and for that excellent reason for which the poet disliked Dr Fell – the appearance of old Banquo, in the same place, in the same armchair, reading the newspaper day after day and evening after evening; of Mr Plodder threading among the coffee-room tables and taking note of every man's dinner; of old General Hawkshaw, who makes that constant noise in the Club, sneezing, coughing, and blowing his nose – all these men, by their various defects or qualities, have driven me half mad at times, and I have thought to myself, Oh that I could go to the Club without seeing Banquo – Oh that Plodder would not come and inspect my mutton chop – Oh that fate would remove Hawkshaw and his pocket handkerchief for ever out of my sight and hearing! Well, August arrives, and one's three men of the sea are off one's shoulders. Mr and Mrs Banquo are at Leamington, the paper says; Mr Plodder is gone to Paris to inspect the dinners at the 'Trois Frères'; and Hawkshaw is coughing away at Brighton, where the sad sea waves murmur before him. The Club is your own. How pleasant it is! You can get the *Globe* and *Standard* now without a struggle; you may see all the Sunday papers; when you dine it is not like dining in a street dinned by the tramp of waiters perpetually passing with clanking dishes of various odours, and jostled by young men who look scowlingly down upon your dinner as they pass with creaking boots. They are all gone – you sit in a vast and agreeable apartment with twenty large servants at your orders – if you were a Duke with a thousand pounds a day you couldn't be better served or lodged. Those men, having nothing else to do, are anxious to prevent your desires and make you happy – the butler bustles about with your pint of wine – if you order a dish, the *chef* himself will probably cook it; what mortal can ask more?

I once read in a book purporting to give descriptions of London, and life and manners, an account of a family in the lower ranks of genteel life, who shut up the front windows of their house, and lived in the back rooms, from which they only issued for fresh air surreptitiously at midnight, so that their friends might suppose that they were out of town. I suppose that there is some foundation for this legend. I suppose that some people *are* actually afraid to be seen in

London, when the persons who form their society have quitted the metropolis: and that Mr and Mrs Higgs being left at home at Islington, when Mr and Mrs Biggs, their next door neighbours, have departed for Margate or Gravesend, feel pangs of shame at their own poverty, and envy at their friends' better fortune. I have seen many men and cities, my dear Bob, and noted their manners: and for servility I will back a free-born Englishman of the respectable classes against any man of any nation in the world. In the competition for social rank between Higgs and Biggs, think what a strange standard of superiority is set up! – a shilling steamer to Gravesend, and a few shrimps more or less on one part or the other, settle the claim. Perhaps in what is called high life, there are disputes as paltry, aims as mean, and distinctions as absurd: but my business is with this present folly of being ashamed to be in London. Ashamed, sir! I like being in London at this time, and have so much to say regarding the pleasures of the place in the dead season, that I hope to write you another letter regarding it next week.

II

areering during the season from one party to another, from one great dinner of twenty covers to another of eighteen guests; from Lady Hustlebury's rout to Mrs Packington's soirée – friendship, to a man about town, becomes impossible from February to August: it is only his acquaintances he can cultivate during those six months of turmoil.

In the last fortnight, one has had leisure to recur to more tender emotions: in other words, as nobody has asked me to dinner, I have been about seeking dinners from my old friends. And very glad are they to see you: very kindly and hospitable are they disposed to be, very pleasant are those little calm *réunions* in the quiet summer evenings, when the beloved friend of your youth and you sip a bottle of claret together leisurely without candles, and ascend to the drawing-room where the friend of your youth's wife sits blandly presiding over the teapot. What matters that it is the metal teapot, the silver utensils being packed off to the banker's? What matters that the hangings are down, and the lustre in a brown-holland bag? Intimacy increases by this artless confidence – you are admitted to a family *en déshabille*. In an honest man's house, the wine is never sent to the banker's; he can always go to the cellar for that. And so we drink and prattle in quiet – about the past season, about our sons at college, and what not. We become intimate again, because Fate, which has long separated us, throws us once more together. I say the dull season is a kind season: gentle and amiable, friendly and full of quiet enjoyment.

Among these pleasant little meetings, for which the present season has given time and opportunity, I shall mention one, sir, which took place last Wednesday, and which during the very dinner itself I vowed I would describe, if the venerable *Mr Punch* would grant me leave and space, in the columns of a journal which has for its object the promotion of mirth and goodwill.

In the year eighteen hundred and something, sir, there lived at a villa, at a short distance from London, a certain gentleman and lady who had many acquaintances and friends, among whom was your humble servant. For to become acquainted with this young woman was to be her friend, so friendly was she, so kind, so gentle, so full of natural genius, and graceful feminine accomplishment. Whatever she did, she did charmingly; her life was decorated with a hundred pretty gifts, with which, as one would fancy, kind fairies had endowed her cradle; music and pictures seemed to flow naturally out of her hand, as she laid it on the piano or the drawing-board. She sang exquisitely, and with a full heart, and as if she couldn't help it any more than a bird. I have an image of this fair creature before me now, a calm, sunshiny evening, a green lawn flaring with roses and geraniums, and a half-dozen gentlemen sauntering thereon in a state of great contentment, or gathered under the verandah, by the open French window: near by she sits singing at the piano. She is in a pink dress: she has *gigot* sleeves; a little child in a prodigious sash is playing about at her mother's knee. She sings song after song; the sun goes down behind the black fir trees that belt the lawn, and Missy in the blue sash vanishes to the nursery; the room darkens in the twilight; the stars appear in the heaven – and the tips of the cigars glow on the balcony: she sings song after song, in accents soft and low, tender and melodious – we are never tired of hearing her. Indeed, Bob, I can hear her still –

the stars of those calm nights still shine in my memory, and I have been humming one of her tunes with my pen in my mouth, to the surprise of Mr Dodder, who is writing at the opposite side of the table, and wondering at the lackadaisical expression which pervades my venerable mug.

You will naturally argue from the above pathetic passage, that I was greatly smitten by Mrs Nightingale (as we will call this lady, if you will permit me). You are right, sir. For what is an amiable woman made, but that we should fall in love with her? I do not mean to say that you are to lose your sleep, or give up your dinner, or make yourself unhappy in her absence; but when the sun shines (and it is not too hot) I like to bask in it: when the bird sings, to listen: and to admire that which is admirable with an honest and hearty enjoyment. There were a half-dozen men at the period of which I speak who wore Mrs Nightingale's colours, and we used to be invited down from London of a Saturday and Sunday, to Thornwood, by the hospitable host and hostess there, and it seemed like going back to school, when we came away by the coach of a Monday morning: we talked of her all the way back to London, to separate upon our various callings when we got into the smoky city. Salvator Rodgers, the painter, went to his easel; Woodward, the barrister, to his chambers; Piper, the doctor, to his patient (for he then had only one), and so forth. Fate called us each to his business, and has sent us upon many a distant errand since that day. But from that day to this, whenever we meet, the remembrance of the holidays at Thornwood has been always a bond of union between us: and we have always had Mrs Nightingale's colours put away amongst the cherished relics of old times.

N was a West India merchant, and his property went to the bad. He died at Jamaica. Thornwood was let to other people, who knew us not. The widow with a small jointure retired, and educated her daughter abroad. We had not heard of her for years and years, nor until she came to town about a legacy a few weeks since.

In those years and years what changes have taken place! Sir Salvator Rodgers is a Member of the Royal Academy; Woodward, the barrister, has made a fortune at the Bar; and in seeing Doctor Piper in his barouche, as he rolls about Belgravia and Mayfair, you at once know what a man of importance he has become.

On last Monday week, sir, I received a letter in a delicate female handwriting, with which I was not acquainted, and which Miss Flora, the landlady's daughter, condescended to bring me, saying that it had been left at the door by two ladies in a brougham.

'— Why did you not let them come upstairs?' said I in a rage, after reading the note.

'We don't know what sort of people goes about in broughams,' said Miss Flora, with a toss of her head; 'we don't want no ladies in *our* house.' And she flung her impertinence out of the room.

The note was signed Frances Nightingale – whereas *our* Nightingale's name was Louisa. But this Frances was no other than the little thing in the large blue sash, whom we remembered at Thornwood ever so many years ago. The writer declared that she recollected me quite well, that her mamma was most anxious to see an old friend, and that they had apartments at No. 166, Clarges Street, Piccadilly, whither I hastened off to pay my respects to Mrs Nightingale.

When I entered the room, a tall and beautiful young woman with blue eyes, and a serene and majestic air, came up to shake hands with me: and I beheld in her, without in the least recognizing, the little Fanny of the blue sash. Mamma came out of the adjoining apartment presently. We had not met since – since all sorts of events had occurred – her voice was not a little agitated. Here was that fair creature whom we had admired so. Sir, I shall not say whether she was altered or not. The tones of her voice were as sweet and kind as ever: – and we talked about Miss Fanny as a subject in common between us, and I admired the growth and beauty of the young lady, though I did not mind telling her to her face (at which to be sure the girl was delighted), that she never in my eyes would be half so pretty as her mother.

Well, sir, upon this day arrangements were made for the dinner which took place on Wednesday last, and to the remembrance of which I determined to consecrate this present page.

It so happened that everybody was in town of the old set of whom I have made mention, and everybody was disengaged.

Sir Salvator Rodgers (who has become such a swell since he was knighted and got the cordon of the Order of the George and Blue Boar of Russia, that we like to laugh at him a little), made his appearance at eight o'clock, and was perfectly natural and affable. Woodward, the lawyer, forgot his abominable law and his money about which he is always thinking: and finally, Doctor Piper, of whom we despaired because his wife is mortally jealous of every lady whom he attends, and will hardly let him dine out of her sight, had pleaded Lady Rackstraw's situation as a reason for not going down to Wimbledon Common till night – and so we six had a meeting.

The door was opened to us by a maid, who looked us hard in the face as we went upstairs, and who was no other than little Fanny's nurse in former days, come like us to visit her old mistress. We all knew her except Woodward, the lawyer, and all shook hands with her except him. Constant study had driven her out of the lawyer's memory. I don't think he ever cared for Mrs Nightingale as much as the rest of us did, or indeed that it is in the nature of that learned man to care for any but one learned person.

And what do you think, sir, this dear and faithful widow had done to make us welcome? She remembered the dishes that we used to like ever so long ago, and she had every man's favourite dish for him. Rodgers used to have a passion for herrings – there they were; the lawyer, who has an enormous appetite, which he gratifies at other people's expense, had a shoulder of mutton and onion sauce, which the lean and hungry man devoured almost entirely: mine did not come till the second course – it was baked plum pudding – I was affected when I saw it, sir – I choked almost when I ate it. Piper made a beautiful little speech, and made an ice compound, for which he was famous, and we drank it just as we used to drink it in old times, and to the health of the widow.

How should we have had this dinner, how could we all have assembled together again, if everybody had not been out of town, and everybody had not been disengaged? Just for one evening, the scattered members of an old circle of friendship returned and met round the old table again – round this little green island we moor for the night at least, – tomorrow we part company, and each man for himself sails over the *ingens aequor*.

Since I wrote the above, I find that everybody really *is* gone away. The widow left town on Friday. I have been on my round just now, and have been met at every step by closed shutters and the faces of unfamiliar charwomen. No. 9 is gone to Malvern. Nos. 37, 15, 25, 48 and 36A, are gone to Scotland. The solitude of the Club begins to be unbearable, and I found Muggins this morning preparing a mysterious apparatus of travelling boot-trees, and dusting the portmanteaus.

If you are not getting on well with the Kickleburys at Homburg I recommend you to go to Spa. Mrs Nightingale is going thither, and will be at the Hôtel d'Orange; where you may use my name and present yourself to her; and I may hint to you in confidence that Miss Fanny will have a very pretty little fortune.

THE PROSER

ESSAYS AND DISCOURSES BY DR SOLOMON PACIFICO

ON A LADY IN AN OPERA-BOX

I

Going the other night to the Conservatoire at Paris, where there was a magnificent assemblage of rank and fashion gathered together to hear the delightful performance of Madame Sontag, the friend who conferred upon me the polite favour of a ticket to the stalls, also pointed out to me who were the most remarkable personages round about us. There were ambassadors, politicians, and gentlemen, military and literary; there were beauties, French, Russian and English: there were old ladies who had been beauties once, and who, by the help of a little distance and politeness (and if you didn't use your opera-glass, which is a cruel detector of paint and wrinkles), looked young and handsome still: and plenty of old bucks in the stalls and boxes, well wigged, well gloved, and brilliantly waistcoated, very obsequious to the ladies, and satisfied with themselves and the world.

Up in the second tier of boxes I saw a very stout, jolly, good-humoured-looking lady, whose head-dress and ringlets and general appurtenances were unmistakably English – and whom, were you to meet her at Timbuctoo, or in the Seraglio of the Grand Sultan amongst a bevy of beauties collected from all the countries of the earth, one would instantly know to be a British female. I do not mean to say that, were I the Padishah, I would select that moon-faced houri out of all the lovely society, and make her the Empress or Grand Signora of my dominions; but simply that there *is* a character about our countrywomen which leads one to know, recognize, and admire, and wonder at them among all women of all tongues and countries. We have our British Lion; we have our Britannia ruling the waves; we have our British female – the most respectable, the most remarkable, of the women of this world. And now we have come to the woman who gives the subject, though she is not herself the subject, of these present remarks.

As I looked at her with that fond curiosity and silent pleasure and wonder which she (I mean the Great British female) always inspires in my mind, watching her smiles, her ways and motions, her allurements and attractive gestures – her head bobbing to this friend whom she recognized in the stalls – her jolly fat hand wagging a welcome to that acquaintance in a neighbouring box – my friend and guide for the evening caught her eye, and made her a respectful bow, and said to me with a look of much meaning, 'That is Mrs Trotter-Walker.' And from that minute I forgot Madame Sontag, and thought only of Mrs T-W.

'So that,' said I, 'is Mrs Trotter-Walker! You have touched a chord in my heart. You have brought back old times to my memory, and made me recall some of the griefs and disappointments of my early days.'

'Hold you tongue, man!' says Tom, my friend. 'Listen to the Sontag; how divinely she is singing! how fresh her voice is still!'

I looked up at Mrs Walker all the time with unabated interest. 'Madam,' thought I, 'you look to be as kind and good natured a person as eyes ever lighted upon. The way in which you are smiling to that young dandy with the double eyeglass, and the *empressement* with which he returns the salute, show that your friends are persons of rank and elegance, and that you are esteemed by them – giving them, as I am sure from your kind appearance you do, good dinners and pleasant balls. But I wonder what would you think if you knew that I was looking at you? I behold you for the first time: there are a hundred pretty young girls in the house, whom an amateur of mere beauty would examine with much greater satisfaction than he would naturally bestow upon a lady whose prime is past; and yet the sight of you interests me, and tickles me, so to speak, and my eyeglass can't remove itself from the contemplation of your honest face.'

What is it that interests me so? What do you suppose interests a man the most in this life? Himself, to be sure. It is at himself he is looking through his opera-glass – himself who is concerned, or he would not be watching you so keenly. And now let me confess why it is that the lady in the upper box excites me so, and why I say, 'That is Mrs Trotter-Walker, is it?' with an air of such deep interest.

Well then. In the year eighteen hundred and thirty odd, it happened that I went to pass the winter at Rome, as we will call the city. Major-General and Mrs Trotter-Walker were also there; and until I heard of them there, I had never heard that there were such people in existence as the General and the lady – the lady yonder with the large fan in the upper boxes. Mrs Walker, as became her station in life, took, I dare say, very comfortable lodgings, gave dinners and parties to her friends, and had a night in the week for receptions.

Much as I have travelled and lived abroad, these evening *réunions* have never greatly fascinated me. Man cannot live upon lemonade, wax-candles, and weak tea. Gloves and white neckcloths cost money, and those plaguy shiny boots are always so tight and hot. Am I made of money, that I can hire a coach to go to one of these *soirées* on a rainy Roman night; or can I come in goloshes, and take them off in the ante-chamber? I am too poor for cabs, and too vain for goloshes. If it had been to see the girl of my heart, (I mean at the time when there were girls, and I had a heart), I couldn't have gone in goloshes. Well, not being in love, and not liking weak tea and lemonade, I did not go to evening parties that year at Rome: nor, of later years, at Paris, Vienna, Copenhagen, Islington, or wherever I may have been.

What, then, were my feelings when my dear and valued friend, Mrs Coverlade, (she is a daughter of that venerable Peer, the Right Honourable the Lord Commandine), who was passing the winter too at Rome, said to me, 'My dear Doctor Pacifico, what have you done to offend Mrs Trotter-Walker?'

'I know no person of that name,' I said. 'I knew Walker of the Post Office, and poor Trotter who was a captain in our regiment, and died under my hands at the Bahamas. But with the Trotter-Walkers I haven't the honour of an acquaintance.'

'Well, it is not likely that you will have that honour,' Mrs Coverlade said. 'Mrs Walker said last night that she did not wish to make your acquaintance, and that she did not intend to receive you.'

'I think she might have waited until I asked her, Madam,' I said, 'What have I done to her? I have never seen or heard of her: how should I want to get into her house? or attend at her Tuesdays – confound her Tuesdays!' I am sorry to say I said, 'Confound Mrs Walker's Tuesdays', and the conversation took another turn, and it so happened that I was called away from Rome suddenly, and never set eyes upon Mrs Walker, or indeed thought about her from that day to this.

Strange endurance of human vanity! a million of much more important conversations have escaped one since then, most likely – but the memory of this little mortification (for such it is, after all) remains quite fresh in the mind, and unforgotten, though it is a trifle, and more than half a score of years old. We forgive injuries, we survive even our remorse for great wrongs that we ourselves commit; but I doubt if we ever forgive slights of this nature put upon us, or forget circumstances in which our self-love had been made to suffer.

Otherwise, why should the remembrance of Mrs Trotter-Walker have remained so lively in this bosom? Why should her appearance have excited such a keen interest in these eyes? Had Venus or Helen (the favourite beauty of Paris) been at the side of Mrs T-W, I should have looked at the latter more than

at the Queen of Love herself. Had Mrs Walker murdered Mrs
Pacifico, or inflicted some mortal injury upon me, I might
forgive her – but for a slight? Never, Mrs Trotter-Walker;
never, by Nemesis, never!

And now, having allowed my personal wrath to explode,
let us calmly moralize for a minute or two upon this little
circumstance; for there is no circumstance, however little, that
won't afford a text for a sermon. Why was it that Mrs General
Trotter-Walker refused to receive Doctor S. Pacifico at her
parties? She had noticed me probably somewhere where I had
not remarked her; she did not like my aquiline countenance,
my manner of taking snuff, my Blucher boots, or what not; or
she had seen me walking with my friend Jack Raggett, the
painter, on the Pincio – a fellow with a hat and beard like a
bandit, a shabby paletot, and a great pipe between his teeth. I
was not genteel enough for her circle – I assume that to be the
reason; indeed, Mrs Coverlade, with a good-natured smile at
my coat, which I own was somewhat shabby, gave me to
understand as much.

You little know, my worthy kind lady, what a loss you had
that season at Rome, in turning up your amiable nose at the
present writer. I could have given you appropriate anecdotes
(with which my mind is stored) of all the courts of Europe
(besides of Africa, Asia, and St Domingo), which I have
visited. I could have made the General die of laughing after
dinner with some of my funny stories, of which I keep a book,
without which I never travel. I am content with my dinner: I
can carve beautifully, and make jokes upon almost any dish at
table. I can talk about wine, cookery, hotels all over the
Continent: – anything you will. I have been familiar with
Cardinals, Red Republicans, Jesuits, German Princes, and
Carbonari; and what is more, I can listen and hold my tongue
in admiration. Ah, Madam! what did you lose in refusing to
make the acquaintance of Solomon Pacifico, M.D.!

And why? Because my coat was a trifle threadbare; because I
dined at the 'Lepre' with Raggett and some of those other
bandits of painters, and had not the money to hire a coach and
horses.

Gentility is the death and destruction of social happiness
amongst the middle classes in England. It destroys naturalness

(if I may coin such a word) and kindly sympathies. The object of life, as I take it, is to be friendly with everybody. As a rule, and to a philosophical cosmopolite, every man ought to be welcome. I do not mean to your intimacy or affection, but to your society; as there is, if we would or could but discover it, something notable, something worthy of observation, of sympathy, of wonder and amusement in every fellow mortal. If I had been Mr Pacifico, travelling with a courier and a carriage, would Mrs Walker have made any objection to me? I think not. It was the Bulcher boots and the worn hat and the homely companion of the individual which were unwelcome to this lady. If I had been disguised Duke of Pacifico, and not a retired army-surgeon, would she have forgiven herself for slighting me? What stores of novels, what *foison* of plays, are composed upon this theme, – the queer old character in the wig and cloak throws off coat and spectacles, and appears suddenly with a star and crown, – a Haroun Alraschid, or other Merry Monarch. And straightway we clap our hands and applaud – what? – the star and garter.

But disguised emperors are not common nowadays. You don't turn away monarchs from your door, any more than angels, unawares. Consider, though, how many a good fellow you may shut out and sneer upon! what an immense deal of pleasure, frankness, kindness, good-fellowship, we forego for the sake of our confounded gentility, and respect for outward show! Instead of placing our society upon an honest footing, we make our aim almost avowedly sordid. Love is of necessity banished from your society when you measure all your guests by a money-standard.

I think of all this – a harmless man – seeing a good natured-looking, jolly woman in the boxes yonder, who thought herself once too great a person to associate with the likes of me. If I give myself airs to my neighbour, may I think of this too, and be a little more humble! And you, honest friend, who read this – have you ever pooh-poohed a man as good as you? If you fall into the society of people whom you are pleased to call your inferiors, did you ever sneer! If so, change I into U, and the fable is narrated for your own benefit, by your obedient servant,

SOLOMON PACIFICO

II

hilst I was riding the other day by the beautiful Serpentine River upon my excellent friend Heaviside's grey cob, and in company of the gallant and agreeable Augustus Toplady, a carriage passed from which looked out a face of such remarkable beauty, that Augustus and myself quickened our pace to follow the vehicle, and to keep for awhile those charming features in view. My beloved and unknown young friend who peruse these lines, it was very likely your face which attracted your humble servant; recollect whether you were not in the Park upon the day I allude to, and if you were, whom else could I mean but you? I don't know your name; I have forgotten the arms on the carriage, or whether there were any; and as for women's dresses, who can remember them? but your dear kind countenance was so pretty and good-humoured and pleasant to look at, that it remains to this day faithfully engraven on my heart, and I feel sure that you are as good as you are handsome. Almost all handsome women are good: they cannot choose but be good and gentle with those sweet features and that charming graceful figure. A day in which one sees a *very* pretty woman should always be noted as a holy day with a man, and marked with a white stone. In this way, and at this season in London, to be sure, such a day comes seven times in the week, and our calendar, like that of the Roman Catholics, is all Saints' days.

Toplady, then, on his chestnut horse, with his glass in his eye, and the tips of his shiny boots just touching the stirrup, and your slave, the present writer, rode after your carriage, and looked at you with such notes of admiration expressed in their eyes, that you remember you blushed, you smiled, and then began to talk to that very nice-looking elderly lady in the front seat, who of course was your Mamma. You turned out of the ride – it was time to go home and dress for dinner, – you were gone. Good luck go with you, and with all fair things which thus come and pass away!

Top caused his horse to cut all sorts of absurd capers and caracoles by the side of your carriage. He made it dance upon two legs, then upon other two, then as if he would jump over the railings and crush the admiring nursery-maids and the rest of the infantry. I should think he got his animal from Batty's, and that, at a crack of Widdicomb's whip, he could dance a quadrille. He ogled, he smiled, he took off his hat to a Countess's carriage that happened to be passing in the other line, and so showed his hair; he grinned, he kissed his little finger-tips and flung them about as if he would shake them off – whereas the other party on the grey cob – the old gentleman – pounded along at a resolute trot, and never once took his respectful eyes off you while you continued in the ring.

When you were gone (you see by the way in which I linger about you still, that I am unwilling to part with you) Toplady turned round upon me with a killing triumphant air, and stroked that impudent little tuft he has on his chin, and said – 'I say, old boy, it was the chestnut she was looking at, and not the *gway*.' And I make no doubt he thinks you are in love with him to this minute.

'You silly young jackanapes,' said I, 'what do I care whether she was looking at the grey or the chestnut? I was thinking about the girl; you were thinking about yourself, and be hanged to your vanity!' And with this thrust in his little chest, I flatter myself I upset young Toplady, that triumphant careering rider.

It was natural that he should wish to please; that is, that he should wish other people to admire him. Augustus Toplady is young (still) and lovely. It is not until a late period of life that a genteel young fellow, with a Grecian nose and a suitable waist and whiskers, begins to admire other people besides himself.

That, however, is the great advantage which a man possesses whose morning of life is over, whose reason is not taken prisoner by any kind of blandishments, and who knows and feels that he is a FOGY. As an old buck is an odious sight, absurd, and ridiculous before gods and men; cruelly, but deservedly, quizzed by you young people, who are not in the least duped by his youthful airs or toilette artifices, so an honest, good-natured, straightforward, middle-aged, easily-pleased Fogy is a worthy and amiable member of society, and a man who gets both respect and liking.

Even in the lovely sex, who has not remarked how painful is that period of a woman's life when she is passing out of her bloom, and thinking about giving up her position as a beauty? What sad injustice and stratagems she has to perpetrate during the struggle! She hides away her daughters in the schoolroom, she makes them wear cruel pinafores, and dresses herself in the garb which they ought to assume. She is obliged to distort the calendar, and to resort to all sorts of schemes and arts to hide, in her own person, the august and respectable marks of time. Ah! what is this revolt against nature but impotent blasphemy? Is not Autumn beautiful in its appointed season, that we are to be ashamed of her and paint her yellowing leaves pea-green? Let us, I say, take the fall of the year as it was made, serenely and sweetly, and await the time when Winter comes and the nights shut in. I know, for my part, many ladies who are far more agreeable and more beautiful too, now that they are no longer beauties; and, by converse, I have no doubt that Toplady, about whom we were speaking just now, will be a far pleasanter person when he has given up the practice, or desire, of killing the other sex, and has sunk into a mellow repose as an old bachelor or a married man.

The great and delightful advantage that a man enjoys in the world, after he has abdicated all pretensions as a conqueror and enslaver of females, and both formally, and of his heart, acknowledges himself to be a Fogy, is that he now comes for the first time to enjoy and appreciate duly the society of women. For a young man about town, there is only one woman in the whole city – (at least very few indeed of the young Turks, let us hope, dare to have two or three strings to their wicked bows) – he goes to ball after ball in pursuit of that one person; he sees no other eyes but hers; hears no other voice; cares for no other petticoat but that in which his charmer dances: he pursues her – is refused – is accepted and jilted; breaks his heart, mends it of course, and goes on again after some other beloved being, until in the order of fate and nature he marries and settles, or remains unmarried, free, and a Fogy. Until then we know nothing of women – the kindness and refinement and wit of the elders; the artless prattle and dear little chatter of the young ones; all these are hidden from us until we take the Fogy's degree: nay, even perhaps from married men, whose age and gravity entitle them to rank amongst Fogies; for every woman, who is worth anything, will be jealous of her husband up to seventy or eighty, and always prevent his intercourse with other ladies. But an old bachelor, or better still, an old widower, has this delightful *entrée* into the female world: he is free to come; to go; to listen; to joke; to sympathize; to talk with mamma about her plans and troubles; to pump from Miss the little secrets that gush so easily from her pure little well of a heart; the ladies do not *gêner* themselves before him, and he is admitted to their mysteries like the Doctor, the Confessor, or the Kislar Aga.

What man, who can enjoy this pleasure and privilege, ought to be indifferent to it? If the society of one woman is delightful, as the young fellows think, and justly, how much more delightful is the society of a thousand! One woman, for instance, has brown eyes, and a geological or musical turn; another has sweet blue eyes, and takes, let us say, the Gorham side of the controversy at present pending; a third darling, with long fringed lashes hiding eyes of hazel, lifts them up ceiling-wards on behalf of Miss Sellon, thinks the Lord Chief Justice has hit the poor young lady very hard in publishing her letters, and proposes to quit the Church next Tuesday or Wednesday, or whenever Mr Oriel is ready – and, of course, a man may be in love with one or the other of these. But it is manifest that brown eyes will remain brown eyes to the end, and that, having no other interest but music or geology, her conversation on those points may grow more than sufficient. Sapphira, again, when she has said her say with regard to the Gorham affair, and proved that the other party are but Romanists in disguise, and who is interested on no other subject, may possibly tire you – so may Hazelia, who is working altar-cloths all day, and would desire no better martyrdom than to walk barefoot in a night procession up Sloane Street and home by Wilton Place, time enough to get her poor *meurtris* little feet into white satin slippers for the night's ball – I say, if a man can be wrought up to rapture, and enjoy bliss in the company of any one of these young ladies, or any other individuals in the infinite variety of Miss-kind – how much real sympathy, benevolent pleasure, and kindly observation may he enjoy, when he is allowed to be familiar with the whole charming race, and behold the brightness of all their different eyes, and listen to the sweet music of their various voices!

ON THE BENEFITS OF BEING A FOGY

III

n possession of the right and privilege of garrulity which is accorded to old age, I cannot allow that a single side of paper should contain all that I have to say in respect to the manifold advantages of being a Fogy. I am a Fogy, and have been a young man. I see twenty women in the world constantly to whom I would like to have given a lock of my hair in days when my pate boasted of that ornament; for whom my heart felt tumultuous emotions, before the victorious and beloved Mrs Pacifico subjugated it. If I had any feelings now, Mrs P would order them and me to be quiet: but I have none; I am tranquil – yes, really tranquil (though as my dear Leonora is sitting opposite to me at this minute, and has an askance glance from her novel to my paper as I write – even if I were *not* tranquil, I should say that I was; but I *am* quiet): I have passed the hot stage: and I do not know a pleasanter and calmer feeling of mind than that of a respectable person of the middle age, who can still be heartily and generously fond of all the women whom he was in a passion and a fever in early life. If you cease liking a woman when you cease loving her, depend on it that one of you is a bad one. You are parted, never mind with what pangs on either side, or by what circumstances of fate, choice, or necessity, – you have no money or she has too much, or she likes somebody else better, and so forth; but an honest Fogy should always, unless reason be given to the contrary, think well of the woman whom he has once thought well of, and remember her with kindness and tenderness, as a man remembers a place where he has been very happy.

A proper management of his recollections thus constitutes a very great item in the happiness of a Fogy. I, for my part, would rather remember —, and —, and — (I dare not mention names, for isn't my Leonora pretending to read 'The Initials', and peeping over my shoulder?) than be in love over again. It is because I have suffered prodigiously from that passion that I am interested in beholding others undergoing the malady. I watch it in all ballrooms (over my cards, where I and the old ones sit), and dinner-parties. Without sentiment, there would be no flavour in life at all. I like to watch young folks who are fond of each other, be it the housemaid furtively engaged smiling and glancing with John through the area railings; be it Miss and the Captain whispering in the embrasure of the drawing-room window – *Amant* is interesting to me because of *Amavi* – of course it is Mrs Pacifico I mean.

All Fogies of good breeding and kind condition of mind, who go about in the world much, should remember to efface themselves – if I may use a French phrase – they should not, that is to say, thrust in their old mugs on all occasions. When the people are marching out to dinner, for instance, and the Captain is sidling up to Miss, Fogy, because he is twenty years older than the Captain, should not push himself forward to arrest that young fellow, and carry off the disappointed girl on his superannuated rheumatic old elbow. When there is anything of this sort going on (and a man of the world has possession fo the *carte du pays* with half an eye), I become interested in a picture, or have something particular to say to pretty Polly the parrot, or to little Tommy, who is not coming in to dinner, and while I am talking to him, Miss and the Captain make their little arrangement. In this way I managed only last week to let young Billington and the lovely Blanche Pouter get together; and walked downstairs with my hat for the only partner of my arm. Augustus Toplady now, because he was a Captain of Dragoons almost before

Billington was born, would have insisted upon his right of precedence over Billington, who only got his troop the other day.

Precedence! Fiddlestick! Men squabble about precedence because they are doubtful about their condition, as Irishmen will insist upon it that you are determined to insult and trample upon their beautiful country, whether you are thinking about it or no; men young to the world mistrust the bearing of others towards them, because they mistrust themselves. I have seen many sneaks and much cringing of course in the world; but the fault of gentlefolks is generally the contrary – an absurd doubt of the intentions of others towards us, and a perpetual assertion of our twopenny dignity, which nobody is thinking of wounding.

As a young man, if the Lord I knew did not happen to notice me, the next time I met him I used to envelope myself in my dignity, and treat his Lordship with such a tremendous *hauteur* and killing coolness of demeanour, that you might have fancied I was an Earl at least, and he a menial upon whom I trampled. Whereas he was a simple, good-natured creature who had no idea of insulting or slighting me, and, indeed, scarcely any idea about any subject, except racing and shooting. Young men have this uneasiness in society, because they are thinking about themselves: Fogies are happy and tranquil, because they are taking advantage of, and enjoying, without suspicion, the good-nature and good offices of other well-bred people.

Have you often wished for yourself, or some other dear friend, ten thousand a year? It is natural that you should like such a good thing as ten thousand a year; and all the pleasures and comforts which it brings. So also it is natural that a man should like the society of people well-to-do in the world; who make their houses pleasant, who gather pleasant persons about them, who have fine pictures on their walls, pleasant books in their libraries, pleasant parks and town and country houses, good cooks and good cellars; if I were coming to dine with you, I would rather have a good dinner than a bad one; if so-and-so is as good as you and possesses these things, he, in so far, is better than you who do not possess them: therefore I had rather go to his house in Belgravia than to your lodgings in Kentish Town. That is the rationale of living in good company. An absurd, conceited, high-and-mighty young man hangs back, at once insolent and bashful; and honest, simple, quiet, easy, clear-sighted Fogy steps in and takes the goods which the gods provide, without elation as without squeamishness.

It is only a few men who attain simplicity in early life. This man has his conceited self-importance to be cured of; that has his conceited bashfulness to be 'taken out of him', as the phrase is. You have a disquiet which you try to hide, and you put on a haughty guarded manner. You are suspicious of the goodwill of the company round about you, or of the estimation in which they hold you. You sit mum at table. It is not your place to 'put yourself forward'. You are thinking about yourself, that is; you are suspicious about that personage and everybody else; that is, you are not frank; that is, you are not well-bred; that is, you are not agreeable. I would instance my young friend Mumford as a painful example – one of the wittiest, cheeriest, cleverest, and most honest of fellows in his own circle; but having the honour to dine the other day at Mr Hobanob's, where his Excellency the Crimean Minister and several gentlemen of humour and wit were assembled, Mumford did not open his mouth once for the purposes of conversation, but sat and ate his dinner as silently as a brother of La Trappe.

He was thinking with too much distrust of himself (and of others by consequence), as Toplady was thinking of himself in the little affair in Hyde Park to which I have alluded in the former chapter. When Mumford is an honest Fogy, like some folks, he will neither distrust his host, nor his company, nor himself; he will make the best of the hour and the people round about him; he will scorn tumbling over head and heels for his dinner, but he will take and give his part of the good things, join in the talk and laugh unaffectedly, nay, actually tumble over head and heels, perhaps, if he has a talent that way; not from a wish to show off his powers, but from a sheer good humour and desire to oblige. Whether as guest or as entertainer, your part and business in society is to make people as happy and as easy as you can; the master gives you his best wine and welcome – you give, in your turn, a smiling face, a disposition to be pleased and to please; and my good young friend who read this, don't doubt about yourself, or think about your precious person. When you have got on your best coat and waistcoat, and have your dandy shirt and tie arranged – consider these as so many settled things, and go forward and through your business.

That is why people in what is called the great world are commonly better bred than persons less fortunate in their condition: not that they are better in reality, but from circumstances they are never uneasy about their position in the world: therefore they are more honest and simple: therefore they are better bred than Growler, who scowls at the great man a defiance and a determination that he will *not* be trampled upon': or poor Fawner, who goes quivering down on his knees, and licks my lord's shoes. But I think in our world – at least in my experience – there are even more Growlers than Fawners.

It will be seen by the above remark, that a desire to shine or to occupy a marked place in society does not constitute my idea of happiness, or become the character of a discreet Fogy. Time, which has dimmed the lustre of his waistcoats, allayed the violence of his feelings, and sobered down his head with grey, should give to the whole of his life a quiet neutral tinge; out of which calm and reposeful condition an honest old Fogy looks on the world, and the struggle there of women and men. I doubt whether this is not better than struggling yourself, for you preserve your interest and do not lose your temper. Succeeding? What is the great use of succeeding? Failing? Where is the great harm? It seems to you a matter of vast interest at one time of your life whether you shall be a lieutenant or a colonel – whether you shall or shall not be invited to the Duchess's party – whether you shall get the place you and a hundred other competitors are trying for – whether Miss will have you or not: what the deuce does it all matter a few years afterwards? Do you, Jones, mean to intimate a desire that History should occupy herself with your paltry personality? The Future does not care whether you were a captain or a private soldier. You get a card to the Duchess's party: it is no more or less than a ball, or a breakfast, like other balls or breakfasts. You are half-distracted because Miss won't have you and takes the other fellow, or you get her (as I did Mrs Pacifico) and find that she is quite a different thing from what you expected. Psha! These things appear as nought – when Time passes – Time the consoler – Time the anodyne – Time the grey calm satirist, whose sad smile seems to say, Look, O man, at the vanity of the objects you pursue, and of yourself who pursue them!

But on the one hand, if there is an alloy in all success, is there not a something wholesome in all disappointment? To endeavour to regard them both benevolently, is the task of a philosopher; and he who can do so is a very lucky Fogy.

ON A GOOD-LOOKING YOUNG LADY

IV

ome time ago I had the fortune to witness at the house of Erminia's brother a rather pretty and affecting scene: whereupon, as my custom is, I would like to make a few moral remarks. I must premise that I knew Erminia's family long before the young lady was born. Victorina her mother, Boa her aunt, Chinchilla her grandmother – I have been intimate with every one of these ladies: and at the table of Sabilla, her married sister, with whom Erminia lives, have a cover laid for me whenever I choose to ask for it.

Everybody who has once seen Erminia remembers her. Fate is beneficent to a man before whose eyes at the parks, or churches, or theatres, or public or private assemblies it throws Erminia. To see her face is a personal kindness for which one ought to be thankful to Fortune; who might have shown you Caprella, with her whiskers, or Felissa, with her savage eyes, instead of the calm and graceful, the tender and beautiful

Erminia. When she comes into the room, it is like a beautiful air of Mozart breaking upon you: when she passes through a ballroom, everybody turns and asks who is that Princess, that fairy lady? Even the women, especially those who are the most beautiful themselves, admire her. By one of those kind freaks of favouritism which Nature takes, she has endowed this young lady with almost every kind of perfection: has given her a charming face, a perfect form, a pure heart, a fine perception and wit, a pretty sense of humour, a laugh and a voice that are as sweet as music to hear, for innocence and tenderness ring in every accent, and a grace of movement which is a curiosity to watch, for in every attitude of motion or repose her form moves or settles into beauty, so that a perpetual grace accompanies her. I have before said that I am an old fogy. On the day when I leave off admiring, I hope I shall die. To see Erminia, is not to fall in love with her: there are some women too handsome, as it were, for that: and I would as soon think of making myself miserable because I could not marry the moon, and make the silver-bowed Goddess Diana Mrs Pacifico, as I should think of having any personal aspirations towards Miss Erminia.

Well then, it happened the other day that this almost peerless creature, on a visit to the country, met that great poet, Timotheus, whose habitation is not far from the country house of Erminia's friend, and who, upon seeing the young lady, felt for her that admiration which every man of taste experiences upon beholding her, and which, if Mrs Timotheus had not been an exceedingly sensible person, would have caused a jealousy between her and the great bard her husband. But, charming and beautiful herself, Mrs Timotheus can even pardon another woman for being so; nay, with perfect good sense, though possibly with a *little* factitious enthusiasm, she professes to share to its fullest extent the admiration of the illustrious Timotheus for the young beauty.

After having made himself well acquainted with Erminia's perfections, the famous votary of Apollo and leader of the tuneful choir, did what might be expected from such a poet under such circumstances, and began to sing. This is the way in which Nature has provided that poets should express their emotions. When they see a beautiful creature they straightway fall to work with their ten syllables and eight syllables, with duty rhyming to beauty, vernal to eternal, riddle to fiddle, or what you please, and turn out to the best of their ability, and with great pains and neatness on their own part, a copy of verses in praise of the adorable object. I myself may have a doubt about the genuineness of the article produced, or of the passion which vents itself in this way, for how can a man who has to assort carefully his tens and eights, to make his epithets neat and melodious, to hunt here and there for rhymes, and to bite the tip of his pen, or pace the gravel walk in front of his house searching for ideas – I doubt, I say, how a man who must go through the above process before turning out a decent set of verses, can be actuated by such strong feelings as you and I, when, in the days of our youth, with no particular preparation, but with our hearts full of manly ardour, and tender and respectful admiration, we went to the Saccharissa for the time being, and poured out our souls at her feet. That sort of eloquence comes spontaneously; that poetry doesn't require rhyme-jingling and metre-sorting, but rolls out of you you don't know how, as much, perhaps, to your own surprise as to that of the beloved object whom you address. In my time, I know whenever I began to make verses about a woman, it was when my heart was no longer very violently smitten about her, and the verses were a sort of mental dram and artificial stimulus with which a man worked himself up to represent enthusiasm and perform passion. Well, well; I see what you mean; I *am* jealous of him. Timotheus's verses were beautiful, that's the fact – confound him! – and I wish I could write as well, or half as well indeed, or do anything to give Erminia pleasure. Like an honest man and faithful servant, he went and made the best thing he could, and laid his offering at Beauty's feet. What can a gentleman do more? My dear Mrs Pacifico here remarks that I never made *her* a copy of verses. Of course not, my love. I am not a verse-making man, nor are you that sort of object – that sort of target, I may say – at which, were I a poet, I would choose to discharge those winged shafts of Apollo.

When Erminia got the verses and read them, she laid them down, and with one of the prettiest and most affecting emotions which I ever saw in my life, she began to cry a little.

The verses of course were full of praises of her beauty. 'They all tell me that,' she said; 'nobody cares for anything but that,' cried the gentle and sensitive creature, feeling within that she had a thousand accomplishments, attractions, charms, which her hundred thousand lovers would not see, whilst they were admiring her mere outward figure and headpiece.

I once heard of another lady, '*de par le monde*', as honest Des Bourdeilles says, who after looking at her plain face in the glass, said, beautifully and pathetically, 'I am sure I should have made a good wife to any man, if he could but have got over my face!' and bewailing her maidenhood in this touching and artless manner, saying that she had a heart full of love, if anybody would accept it, full of faith and devotion, could she but find some man on whom to bestow it; she but echoed the sentiment which I have mentioned above, and which caused in the pride of her beauty the melancholy of the lonely and victorious beauty. 'We are full of love and kindness, ye men!' each says; 'of truth and purity. We don't care about *your* good looks. Could we but find the right man, the man who loved us for ourselves, we would endow him with all the treasures of our hearts, and devote our lives to make him happy.' I admire and reverence Erminia's tears, and the simple heart-stricken plaint of the other forsaken lady. She is Jephthah's daughter condemned by no fault of her own, but doomed by Fate to disappear from among women. The other is a Queen in her splendour to whom all the Lords and Princes bow down and pay worship. 'Ah!' says she, 'it is to the Queen you are kneeling, all of you. I am a woman under this crown and this ermine. I want to be loved, and not to be worshipped: and to be allowed to love is given to everybody but me.'

How much finer a woman's nature is than a man's (by an Ordinance of Nature for the purpose no doubt devised), how much purer and less sensual than ours, is seen in that fact so consoling to misshapen men, to ugly men, to little men, to giants, to old men, to poor men, to men scarred with the smallpox, or ever so ungainly or unfortunate – that their ill-looks or mishaps don't influence women regarding them, and that the awkwardest fellow has a chance for a prize. Whereas, when we, brutes that we are, enter a room, we sidle up naturally towards the prettiest woman; it is the pretty face and figure which attracts us; it is not virtue, or merit, or mental charms, be they ever so great. When one reads the fairy tale of Beauty and the Beast, no one is at all surprised at Beauty's being moved by Beast's gallantry, and devotion, and true-heartedness, and rewarding him with her own love at last. There was hardly any need to make him a lovely young Prince in a gold dress under his horns and bearskin. Beast as he was, but good Beast, loyal Beast, brave, affectionate, upright, generous, enduring Beast, she would have loved his ugly mug without any attraction at all. It is her nature to do so, God bless her! It was a man made the story, one of those twopenny-halfpenny men-milliner moralists, who think that to have a handsome person and a title are the greatest gifts of fortune, and that a man is not complete unless he is a lord and has glazed boots. Or it may have been that the transformation alluded to did not actually take place, but was only spiritual, and in Beauty's mind, and that, seeing before her loyalty, bravery, truth, and devotion, they became in her eyes lovely, and that she hugged her Beast with a perfect contentment to the end.

When ugly Wilkes said that he was only a quarter of an hour behind the handsomest man in England; meaning that the charms of his conversation would make him in that time at a lady's side as agreeable and fascinating as a beau, what a compliment he paid the whole sex! How true it is (not of course applicable to *you*, my dear reader and lucky dog who possess both wit and the most eminent personal attractions, but of the world in general), *We* look for Beauty: women for Love.

So, fair Erminia, dry your beautiful eyes and submit to your lot, and to that adulation which all men pay you; in the midst of which court of yours the sovereign must perforce be lonely. That solitude is a condition of your life, my dear young lady, which many would like to accept, nor will your dominion last much longer than my Lord Farncombe's, let us say, at the Mansion House, whom Time and the inevitable November will depose. Another potentate will ascend his throne: the toast-master will proclaim another name than his, and the cup will be pledged to another health. As with Xerxes and all his courtiers and army at the end of a few years, as with the flowers of the field, as with Lord Farncombe, so with Erminia: were I Timotheus of the tuneful quire, I might follow out this simile between Lord Mayors and Beauties, and with smooth rhymes and quaint antithesis make a verse offering to my fair young lady. But, Madam, your faithful Pacifico is not a poet, only a proser: and it is in truth, and not in numbers, that he admires you.

V

y rising young friend Hitchings, the author of *Randolph the Robber*, *The Murderers of May Fair*, and other romances, and one of the chief writers in the *Lictor* newspaper – a highly liberal, nay, seven-leagued boots progressional journal, was discoursing with the writer of the present lines upon the queer decision to which the French Assembly has come, and which enforces a signature henceforth to all the leading articles in the French papers. As an act of Government, Hitchings said he thought the measure most absurd and tyrannous, but he was not sorry for it, as it would infallibly increase the importance of the profession of letters, to which we both belonged. The man of letters will no longer be the anonymous slave of the newspaper-press proprietor, Hitchings said; the man of letters will no longer be used and flung aside in his old days; he will be rewarded according to his merits, and have the chance of making himself a name. And then Hitchings spoke with great fervour regarding the depressed condition of literary men, and said the time was coming when their merits would get them their own.

On this latter subject, which is a favourite one with many gentlemen of our profession, I, for one, am confessedly incredulous. I am resolved not to consider myself a martyr. I never knew a man who had written a good book (unless, indeed, it were a Barrister with Attorneys), hurt his position in society by having done so. On the contrary, a clever writer, with decent manners and conduct, makes more friends than any other man. And I do not believe (parenthetically) that it will make much difference to my friend Hitchings whether his name is affixed to one, twenty, or two thousand articles of his composition. But what would happen in England if such a regulation as that just passed in France were to become law; and the House of Commons omnipotent, which can shut up our parks for us, which can shut up our Post Office for us, which can do anything it will, should take a fancy to have the signature of every writer of a newspaper article?

Have they got any secret ledger at *The Times* in which the names of the writers of all the articles in that journal are written down? That would be a curious book to see. Articles in that paper have been attributed to every great man of the day: at one time it was said Brougham wrote regularly, at another Canning was a known contributor, at some other time it was Sir Robert Peel, Lord Aberdeen. It would be curious to see the real names. The Chancellor's or the Foreign Secretary's articles would most likely turn out to be writen by Jones or Smith. I mean no disrespect to the latter, but the contrary – to be a writer for a newspaper requires more knowledge, genius, readiness, scholarship, than you want in Saint Stephen's. Compare a good leading article and a speech in the House of Commons: compare a House of Commons orator with a writer, psha!

Would Jones or Smith, however, much profit by the publication of their names to their articles? That is doubtful. When the *Chronicle* or the *Times* speaks now, it is 'we' who are speaking, we the Liberal Conservatives, we the Conservative Sceptics; when Jones signs the article, it is we no more, but Jones. It goes to the public with no authority. The public does not care very much what Jones's opinions are. They don't purchase the Jones organ anymore – the paper droops; and, in fact, I can conceive nothing more wearisome than to see the names of Smith, Brown, Jones, Robinson, and so forth, written in capitals every day, day after day, under the various articles of the paper. The public would begin to cry out at the poverty of the literary *dramatis personae*. We have had Brown twelve times this month it would say. That Robinson's name is always coming up – as soon as there is a finance question, or a foreign question, or what not it is Smith who signs the article. Give us somebody else.

Thus Brown and Robinson would get a doubtful and precarious bread instead of the comfortable and regular engagement which they now have. The paper would not be what it is. It would be impossible to employ men on trial, and see what their talents were worth. Occasion is half a public writer's battle. To sit down in his study and compose an article that *might* be suitable, is a hard work for him: twice as hard as the real work; and yet not the real work; which is to fight the battle at two hours' notice, at the given place and time. The debate is over at twelve o'clock at night, let us say. Mr Editor looks round, and fixes on his man. 'Now's your time, Captain Smith,' says he, 'charge the enemy, and rout them,' – or 'advance, Colonel Jones, with your column and charge.'

Now there may be men who are Jones's or Robinson's superiors in intellect, and who – give them a week or ten days to prepare – would turn out such an article as neither of the two men named could ever have produced – that is very likely. I have often, for my part, said the most brilliant thing in the world, and one that would utterly upset that impudent Jenkins, whose confounded jokes and puns spare nobody – but then it has been three hours after Jenkins's pun, when I was walking home very likely – and so it is with writers; some of them possess the amazing gift of the impromptu, and can always be counted upon in a moment of necessity – whilst others, slower coaches or leaders, require to get all their heavy guns into position, and laboriously to fortify their camp, before they begin to fire.

Now, saying that Robinson is the fellow chiefly to be intrusted with the quick work of the paper, it would be a most unkind and unfair piece of tyranny on the newspaper proprie-tor to force him to publish Robinson's name as the author of all the articles *d'occasion*. You have no more right to call for this publicity from the newspaper owner, who sells you three yards of this printed fabric, than to demand from the linen draper, from what wholesale house he got his calico; who spun it; who owned the cotton, and who cropped it in America. It is the article, and not the name and pedigree of the artificer, which a newspaper or any other dealer has a right to sell to the public. If I get a letter (which Heaven forbid!) from Mr Tapes my attorney, I know it is not in Tapes's own handwriting; I know it is a clerk writes it – so, a newspaper is a composite work got up by many hireling hands, or whom it is necessary to know no other name than the printer's or proprietor's.

It is not to be denied that men of signal ability will write for years in papers and perish unknown – and in so far their lot is a hard one: and the chances of life are against them. It is hard upon a man, with whose work the whole town is ringing, that not a soul should know or care who is the author who so delights the public.

But, on the other hand, if your article is excellent, would you have had any great renown from it, supposing the paper had not published it? Would you have had a chance at all but for that paper? Suppose you had brought out that article on a broad sheet, who would have bought it? Did you ever hear of an unknown man making a fortune by a pamphlet?

Again, it may so happen to a literary man that the stipend which he receives from one publication is not sufficient to boil his family pot, and that he must write in some other quarter. If Brown writes articles in the daily papers, and articles in the weekly and monthly periodicals too, and signs the same, he surely weakens his force by extending his line. It would be better for him to write incognito, than to placard his name in so many quarters – as actors understand, who do not perform in too many pieces on the same night; and painters, who know that it is not worth their while to exhibit more than a certain number of pictures.

Besides, if to some men the want of publicity is an evil: to many others the privacy is most welcome. Many a young barrister is a public writer, for instance, to whose future prospects his fame as a literary man would give no possible aid, and whose intention it is to put away the pen, when the attorneys begin to find out his juridical merits. To such a man it would only be a misfortune to be known as a writer of leading articles. *His* battle for fame and fortune is to be made with other weapons than the pen. Then again, a man without ambition – and there are very many such sensible persons, or whose ambition does not go beyond his *pot au feu*, is happy to have the opportunity of quietly and honourably adding to his income: of occupying himself: of improving himself: of paying for Tom at college, or for Mamma's carriage – and what not. Take away this modest mask – force every man upon the public stage to appear with his name placarded, and we lose some of the best books, some of the best articles, some of the pleasantest wit that we have ever had.

On the whole, then, in this controversy I am against Hitchings; and although he insists upon it that he is a persecuted being, I do not believe it; and although he delcares that I ought to consider myself trampled on by the world, I decline to admit that I am persecuted, and protest that it treats me and my brethren kindly in the main.

HILD'S
PARTIES:

AND A REMONSTRANCE CONCERNING THEM*

I

Sir, – As your publication finds its way to almost every drawing-room table in this metropolis, and is read by the young and old in every family, I beseech you to give admission to the remonstrance of an unhappy parent, and to endeavour to put a stop to a practice which appears to me to be increasing daily, and is likely to operate most injuriously upon the health, morals, and comfort of society in general.

The awful spread of Juvenile Parties, sir, is the fact to which I would draw your attention. There is no end to those entertainments, and if the custom be not speedily checked, people will be obliged to fly from London at Christmas, and

* Addressed to *Mr Punch*.

hide their children during the holidays. I gave mine warning in a speech at breakfast this day, and said with tears in my eyes that if the Juvenile Party system went on, I would take a house at Margate next winter, for that, by heavens! I could not bear another Juvenile Season in London.

If they would but transfer Innocents' Day to the summer holidays, and let the children have their pleasures in May or June, we might get on. But now in this most ruthless and cut-throat season of sleet, thaw, frost, wind, snow, mud, and sore throats, it is quite a tempting of fate to be going much abroad; and this is the time of all others that is selected for the amusement of our little darlings.

As the first step towards the remedying of the evil of which I complain, I am obliged to look *Mr Punch* himself in his venerable beard, and say, 'You sir, have, by your agents, caused not a little of the mischief. I desire that, during Christmas time at least, Mr Leech should be abolished, or sent to take a holiday. Judging from his sketches, I should say that he must be endowed with a perfectly monstrous organ of philoprogenitiveness; he revels in the delineation of the dearest and most beautiful little boys and girls in turn-down collars and broad sashes, and produces in your *Almanack* a picture of a child's costume ball, in which he has made the little wretches in the dresses of every age, and looking so happy, beautiful, and charming, that I have carefully kept the picture from the sight of the women and children of my own household, and – I will not say burned it, for I had not the heart to do that – but locked it away privately, lest they should conspire to have a costume ball themselves, and little Polly should insist upon appearing in the dress of Anne Boleyne, or little Jacky upon turning out as an Ancient Briton.'

An odious, revolting and disagreeable practice, sir, I say, ought not to be described in a manner so atrociously pleasing. The real satirist has no right to lead the public astray about the Juvenile *Fête* nuisance, and to describe a child's ball as if it was a sort of Paradise, and the little imps engaged as happy and pretty as so many cherubs. They should be drawn, one and all, as hideous – disagreeable – distorted – affected – jealous of each other – dancing awkwardly – with shoes too tight for them – over-eating themselves at supper – very unwell (and deservedly so) the next morning, with Mamma administering a mixture made after the Doctor's prescription, and which should be painted awfully black, in an immense large teacup, and (as might be shown by the horrible expression on the little patient's face) of the most disgusting flavour. Banish, I say, that Mr Leech during Christmas time, at least; for, by a misplaced kindness and absurd fondness for children, he is likely to do them and their parents an incalculable quantity of harm.

As every man, sir, looks at the world out of his own eyes or spectacles, or, in other words, speaks of it as he finds it himself, I will lay before you my own case, being perfectly sure that many another parent will sympathize with me. My family, already inconveniently large, is yet constantly on the increase, and it is out of the question that Mrs Spec* should go to parties, as that admirable woman has the best of occupations at home; where she is always nursing the baby. Hence it becomes the father's duty to accompany his children abroad, and to give them pleasure during the holidays.

Our own place of residence is in South Carolina Place, Clapham Road North, in one of the most healthy of the suburbs of this great City. But our relatives and acquaintances are numerous; and they are spread all over the town and its outskirts. Mrs S has sisters married, and dwelling respectively in Islington, Haverstock Hill, Bedford Place, Upper Baker Street, and Tyburn Gardens; besides the children's grandmother, Kensington Gravel Pits, whose parties we are all of course obliged to attend. A *very* great connection of ours, and *nearly related* to B–r–n–t and MP, lives not a hundred miles from B–lg–ve Square. I could enumerate a dozen more places where our kinsmen or intimate friends are – heads of families every one of them, with their quivers more or less full of little arrows.

What is the consequence? I herewith send it to you in the shape of these eighteen enclosed notes, written in various styles more or less correct and corrected, from Miss Fanny, aged seven, who hopes in round hand, that her dear cousins will come and drink tea with her on New Year's Eve, her

---

* A name sometimes assumed by the writer in his contributions to *Punch*.

birthday, – to that of the Governess of the B–r–n–t in question, who requests the pleasure of our company at a ball, a conjuror, and a Christmas Tree. Mrs Spec, for the valid reason above stated, cannot frequent these meetings: I am the deplorable chaperon of the young people. I am called upon to conduct my family five miles to tea at six o'clock. No count is taken of our personal habits, hours of dinner, or intervals of rest. We are made the victims of an infantile conspiracy, nor will the lady of the house hear of any revolt or denial.

'Why,' says she, with the spirit which becomes a woman and mother, 'you go to your *man's* parties eagerly enough: what an unnatural wretch you must be to grudge your children their pleasures!' She looks round, sweeps all six of them into her arms, whilst the baby on her lap begins to bawl, and you are assailed by seven pairs of imploring eyes, against which there is no appeal. You must go. If you are dying of lumbago, if you are engaged to the best of dinners, if you are longing to stop at home and read Macaulay, you must give up all and go.

And it is not to one party or two, but to almost all. You must go to the Gravel Pits, otherwise the grandmother will cut the children out of her will, and leave her property to her *other* grandchildren. If you refuse Islington, and accept Tyburn Gardens, you sneer at a poor relation, and acknowledge a rich one readily enough. If you decline Tyburn Gardens, you fling away the chances of the poor dear children in life, and the hopes of the cadetship for little Jacky. If you go to Hampstead, having declined Bedford Place, it is because you never refuse an invitation to Hampstead, where they make much of you, and Miss Maria is pretty, (as *you* think, though your wife doesn't), and do not care for the Doctor in Bedford Place. And if you accept Bedford Place, you dare not refuse Upper Baker Street, because there is a coolness between the two families, and you must on no account seem to take part with one or the other.

In this way many a man besides myself, I dare say, finds himself miserably tied down, and a helpless prisoner, like Gulliver in the hands of the Lilliputians. Let us just enumerate a few of the miseries of the pitiable parental slave.

In the first place, examine the question in a pecuniary point of view. The expenses of children's toilets at this present time are perfectly frightful.

My eldest boy, Gustavus, at home from Dr Birch's Academy, Rodwell Regis, wears turquoise studs, fine linen shirts, white waistcoats, and shiny boots: and, when I proposed that he should go to a party in Berlin gloves, asked me if I wished that he should be mistaken for a footman? My second, Augustus, grumbles about getting his elder brother's clothes, nor could he be brought to accommodate himself to Gustavus's waistcoats at all, had not his mother coaxed him by the loan of her chain and watch, which later the child broke after many desperate attempts to wind it up. As for the little fellow, Adolphus, his mother has him attired in a costume partly Scotch, partly Hungarian, mostly buttons, and with a Louis Quatorze hat and scarlet feather, and she curls this child's hair with her own blessed tongs every night.

I wish she would do as much for the girls, though: but no, Monsieur Floridor must do that: and accordingly, every day this season, that abominable little Frenchman, who is, I have no doubt, a Red Republican, and smells of cigars and hair-oil, comes over, and, at a cost of eighteenpence *par tête*, figs out my little creatures' heads with fixature, bandoline, crinoline – the deuce knows what.

The bill for silk stockings, sashes, white frocks, is so enormous, that I have not been able to pay my own tailor these three years.

The bill for flys to 'Amstid and back, to Hizzlington and take up, &c., is fearful. The drivers, in this extra weather, must be paid extra, and they drink extra. Having to go to Hackney in the snow, on the night of the 5th of January, our man was so hopelessly inebriated, that I was compelled to get out and drive myself; and I am now, on what is called Twelfth Day (with, of course, another child's party before me for the evening), writing this from my bed, sir, with a severe cold, a violent toothache, and a most acute rheumatism.

As I hear the knock of our medical man, whom an anxious wife has called in, I close this letter; asking leave, however, if I survive, to return to this painful subject next week. And, wishing you a *merry!* New Year, I have the honour to be, dear *Mr Punch*,

Your constant reader,

SPEC.

CHILD'S PARTIES

II

onceive, sir, that in spite of my warning and entreaty we were invited to no less than three Child's Parties last Tuesday; to two of which a lady in this house, who shall be nameless, desired that her children should be taken. On Wednesday we had Dr Lens's microscope; and on Thursday you were good enough to send me your box for the Haymarket Theatre; and of course Mrs S and the children are extremely obliged to you for the attention. I did not mind the theatre so much. I sat in the back of the box, and fell asleep. I wish there was a room with easy chairs and silence enjoined, whither parents might retire, in the houses where Children's Parties are given. But no – it would be of no use: the fiddling and pianoforte-playing and scuffling and laughing of the children would keep you awake.

I am looking out in the papers for some eligible schools where there shall be no vacations – I can't bear these festivities much longer. I begin to hate children in their evening dresses: when children are attired in those absurd best clothes, what can you expect from them but affectation and airs of fashion? One day last year, sir, having to conduct the two young ladies who then frequented juvenile parties, I found them, upon entering the fly, into which they had preceded me under convoy of their maid – I found them – in what a condition, think you? Why, with the skirts of their stiff muslin frocks actually thrown over their heads, so that they should not crumple in the carriage! A child who cannot go into society but with a muslin frock in this position, I say, had best stay in the nursery in her pinafore. If you are not able to enter the world with your dress in its proper place, I say stay at home. I blushed, sir, to see that Mrs S *didn't* blush when I informed her of this incident, but only laughed in a strange indecorous manner, and said that the girls must keep their dresses neat. – Neatness as much as you please, but I should have thought Neatness would wear her frock in the natural way.

And look at the children when they arrive at their place of destination; what processes of coquetry they are made to go through! They are first carried into a room where there are pins, combs, looking-glasses, and lady's-maids, who shake the children's ringlets out, spread abroad their great immense sashes and ribbons, and finally send them full sail into the dancing-room. With what a monstrous precocity they ogle their own faces in the looking-glasses; I have seen my boys, Gustavus and Adolphus, grin into the glass, and arrange their curls or the ties of their neckcloths with as much eagerness as any grown-up man could show, who was going to pay a visit to the lady of his heart. With what an abominable complacency they get out their little gloves, and examine their silk stockings! How can they be natural or unaffected when they are so preposterously conceited about their fine clothes? The other day we met one of Gus's schoolfellows, Master Chaffers, at a party, who entered the room with a little gibus hat under his arm, and to be sure made his bow with the *aplomb* of a dancing-master of sixty; and my boys, who I suspect envied their comrade the gibus hat, began to giggle and sneer at him; and, further to disconcert him, Gus goes up to him and says, 'Why, Chaffers, you consider yourself a deuced fine fellow, but there's a straw on your trousers.' Why shouldn't there be? And why should that poor little boy be called upon to blush because he came to a party in a hack-cab? I, for my part, ordered the children to walk home on that night, in order to punish them for their pride. It rained. Gus wet and spoiled his shiny boots, Dol got a cold, and my wife scolded me for cruelty.

As to the airs which the wretches give themselves about dancing, I need not enlarge upon them here, for the dangerous artist of the 'Rising Generation' has already taken them in hand. Not that his satire does the children the least good: *they* don't see anything absurd in courting pretty girls, or in asserting the superiority of their own sex over the female. A few nights since, I saw Master Sultan at a juvenile ball, standing at the door of the dancing-room, egregiously displaying his muslin pocket handkerchief, and waving it about as if he was in doubt to which of the young beauties he should cast it. 'Why don't you dance, Master Sultan?' says I. 'My good sir,' he answered, 'just look round at those girls and say if I *can* dance?' *Blasé* and selfish now, what will that boy be, sir, when his whiskers grow?

And when you think how Mrs Mainchance seeks out rich partners for her little boys – how my own admirable Eliza has warned her children – 'My dears, I would rather you should dance with your Brown cousins than your Jones cousins,' who are a little rough in their manners (the fact being, that our sister Maria Jones lives at Islington, while Fanny Brown is an Upper Baker Street lady); – when I have heard my dear wife, I say, instruct our boy, on going to a party at the Baronet's, by no means to neglect his cousin Adeliza, but to dance with her as soon as ever he can engage her – what can I say, sir, but that the world of men and boys is the same – that society is poisoned at its source – and that our little chubby-cheeked cherubim are instructed to be artful and egotistical, when you would think by their faces they were just fresh from heaven.

Among the *very* little children, I confess I get a consolation as I watch them, in seeing the artless little girls walking after the boys to whom they incline, and courting them by a hundred innocent little wiles and caresses, putting out their little hands and inviting them to dances, seeking them out to pull crackers with them, and begging them to read the mottoes, and so forth – this is as it should be – this is natural and kindly. The women, by rights, ought to court the men; and they would if we but left them alone.*

---

* On our friend's manuscript there is written, in a female handwriting, 'Vulgar, immodest. – E.S.'

And, absurd as the games are, I own I like to see some thirty or forty of the creatures on the floor in a ring, playing at *petit jeux*, of all ages and sexes, from the most insubordinate infanthood of Master Jacky, who will crawl out of the circle, and talks louder than anybody in it, though he can't speak, to blushing Miss Lily, who is just conscious that she is sixteen – I own, I say, that I can't look at such a circlet or chaplet of children, as it were, in a hundred different colours, laughing and happy, without a sort of pleasure. How they laugh, how they twine together, how they wave about, as if the wind was passing over the flowers! Poor little buds, shall you bloom long? – (I then say to myself, by way of keeping up a proper frame of mind) – shall frosts nip you, or tempests scatter you, drought wither you, or rain beat you down? And oppressed with my feelings, I go below and get some of the weak negus with which Children's Parties are refreshed.

At those houses where the magic lantern is practised, I still sometimes get a degree of pleasure, by hearing the voices of the children in the dark, and the absurd remarks which they make as the various scenes are presented – as, in the dissolving views, Cornhill changes into Grand Cairo, as Cupid comes down with a wreath, and pops it on to the head of the Duke of Wellington, as Saint Peter's at Rome suddenly becomes illuminated, and fireworks, not the least like real fireworks, begin to go off from Fort St Angelo – it is certainly not unpleasant to hear the '—0's' of the audience, and the little children chattering in the darkness. But I think I used to like the 'Pull devil, pull baker', and the Doctor Syntax of our youth, much better than your new-fangled dissolving views and pyrotechnic imitations.

As for the conjuror, I am sick of him. There is one conjuror I have met so often during this year and the last, that the man looks quite guilty when the folding doors are opened, and he sees my party of children, and myself amongst the seniors in the back rows. He forgets his jokes when he beholds me: his wretched claptraps and waggeries fail him: he trembles, falters, and turns pale.

I on my side too feel reciprocally uneasy. What right have we to be staring that creature out of his silly countenance? Very likely he has a wife and family dependent for their bread upon his antics. I should be glad to admire them if I could; but how do so? When I see him squeeze an orange or a cannonball right away into nothing, as it were, or multiply either into three cannonballs or oranges, I know the others are in his pocket somewhere. I know that he doesn't put out his eye when he sticks the penknife into it: or that after swallowing (as the miserable humbug pretends to do) a pocket handkerchief, he cannot by any possibility convert it into a quantity of coloured wood-shavings. These flimsy articles may amuse children, but not *us*. I think I shall go and sit down below amongst the servants whilst this wretched man pursues his idiotic delusions before the children.

And the supper, sir, of which our darlings arc made to partake. Have they dined? I ask. Do they have a supper at home, and why do not they? Because it is unwholesome. If it is unwholesome, why do they have supper at all? I have mentioned the wretched quality of the negus. How they can administer such stuff to children I can't think. Though only last week I heard a little boy, Master Swilby, at Miss Waters', say that he had drunk nine glasses of it, and eaten I don't know how many tasteless sandwiches and insipid cakes; after which feats he proposed to fight my youngest son.

As for that Christmas Tree, which we have from the Germans – anybody who knows what has happened to *them* may judge what will befall us from following their absurd customs. Are we to put up pine trees in our parlours, with wax candles and *bonbons*, after the manner of the ancient Druids? Are we . . . ?

. . . My dear sir, my manuscript must here abruptly terminate. Mrs S has just come into my study, and my daughter enters, grinning behind her, with twenty-five little notes, announcing that Master and Miss Spec request the pleasure of Miss Brown, Miss F. Brown, and M.A. Brown's company on the 25th instant. There is to be a conjuror in the back drawing-room, a magic lantern in my study, a Christmas Tree in the dining-room, dancing in the drawing-room – 'And, my dear, we can have whist in our bedroom,' my wife says. 'You know we must be civil to those who have been so kind to our darling children.'

SPEC.

THE CURATE'S WALK

I

I t was the third out of the four bell buttons at the door at which my friend the curate pulled; and the summons was answered after a brief interval.

I must premise that the house before which we stopped was No. 14, Sedan Buildings, leading out of Great Guelph Street, Dettingen Street, Culloden Street, Minden Square; and Upper and Lower Caroline Row form part of the same quarter – a very queer and solemn quarter to walk in, I think, and one

which always suggests Fielding's novels to me. I can fancy
Captain Booth strutting out of the very door at which we
were standing, in tarnished lace, with his hat cocked over his
eye, and his hand on his hanger; or Lady Bellaston's chair and
bearers coming swinging down Great Guelph Street, which
we have just quitted to enter Sedan Buildings.

Sedan Buildings is a little flagged square, ending abruptly
with the huge walls of Bluck's Brewery. The houses, by many
degrees smaller than the large decayed tenements in Great
Guelph Street, are still not uncomfortable, although shabby.
There are brass-plates on the doors, two on some of them: or
simple names, as 'Lunt', 'Padgemore', &c. (as if no other
statement about Lunt and Padgemore were necessary at all)
under the bells. There are pictures of mangles before two of
the houses, and a gilt arm with a hammer sticking out from
one. I never saw a Goldbeater. What sort of a being is he that
he always sticks out his ensign in dark, mouldy, lonely,
dreary, but somewhat respectable places? What powerful
Mulciberian fellows they must be, those Goldbeaters,
whacking and thumping with huge mallets at the precious
metals all day. I wonder what is Goldbeaters' skin? and do
they get impregnated with the metal? and are their great arms
under their clean shirts on Sundays, all gilt and shining?

It is a quiet, kind, respectable place somehow, in spite of its
shabbiness. Two pewter pints and a jolly little half-pint are
hanging on the railings in perfect confidence, basking in what
little sun comes into the Court. A group of small children are
making an ornament of oyster shells in one corner. Who has
that half-pint? Is it for one of those small ones, or for some
delicate female recommended to take beer? The windows in
the Court, upon some of which the sun glistens, are not
cracked, and pretty clean; it is only the black and dreary look
behind which gives them a poverty-stricken appearance. No
curtains or blinds. A birdcage and very few pots of flowers
here and there. This – with the exception of a milkman talking
to a whitey-brown woman, made up of bits of flannel and
strips of faded chintz and calico seemingly, and holding a long
bundle which cried – this was all I saw in Sedan Buildings
while we were waiting until the door should open.

At last the door was opened, and by a porteress so small,

that I wonder how she ever could have lifted up the latch. She bobbed a curtsey, and smiled at the Curate, whose face gleamed with benevolence too, in reply to that salutation.

'Mother not at home?' says Frank Whitestock, patting the child on the head.

'Mother's out charing, sir,' replied the girl; 'but please to walk up, sir.' And she led the way up one and two pair of stairs to that apartment in the house which is called the second-floor front; in which was the abode of the charwoman.

There were two young persons in the room, of the respective ages of eight and five, I should think. She of five years of age was hemming a duster, being perched on a chair at the table in the middle of the room. The elder, of eight, politely wiped a chair with a cloth for the accommodation of the good-natured Curate, and came and stood between his knees, immediately alongside of his umbrella, which also reposed there, and which she by no means equalled in height.

'These children attend my school at St Timothy's,' Mr Whitestock said, 'and Betsy keeps the house while her mother is from home.'

Anything cleaner or neater than this house it is impossible to conceive. There was a big bed, which must have been the resting place of the whole of this little family. There were three or four religious prints on the walls; besides two framed and glazed, of Prince Coburg and the Princess Charlotte. There were brass candlesticks, and a lamb on the chimney piece, and a cupboard in the corner, decorated with near half a dozen plates, yellow bowls, and crockery. And on the table there were two or three bits of dry bread, and a jug with water, with which these three young people (it being then nearly three o'clock) were about to take their meal called tea.

That little Betsy who looks so small is nearly ten years old: and has been a mother ever since the age of about five. I mean to say, that her own mother having to go out upon her charing operations, Betsy assumes command of the room during her parent's absence: has nursed her sisters from babyhood up to the present time: keeps order over them, and the house clean as you see it; and goes out occasionally and transacts the family purchases of bread, moist sugar, and mother's tea. They dine upon bread, tea and breakfast upon bread when they have it, or go to bed without a morsel. Their holiday is Sunday, which they spend at Church and Sunday school. The younger children scarcely ever go out, save on that day, but sit sometimes in the sun, which comes in pretty pleasantly: sometimes blue in the cold, for they very seldom see a fire except to hear irons by, when mother has a job of linen to get up. Father was a journeyman bookbinder, who died four years ago, and is buried among thousands and thousands of the nameless dead who lie crowding the black churchyard of St Timothy's parish.

The Curate evidently took especial pride in Victoria, the youngest of these three children of the charwoman, and caused Betsy to fetch a book which lay at the window, and bade her read. It was a Missionary Register which the Curate opened haphazard, and this baby began to read out in an exceedingly clear and resolute voice about –

'The island of Raritongo is the least frequented of all the Caribbean Archipelago. Wankyfungo is at four leagues S.E. by E., and the peak of the crater of Shuagnahua is distinctly visible. The "Irascible" entered Raritongo Bay on the evening of Thursday 29th, and the next day the Rev. Mr Flethers, Mrs Flethers, and their nine children, and Shangpooky, the native converted at Cacabawgo, landed and took up their residence at the house of Ratatatua, the Principal Chief, who entertained us with yams and a pig,' &c. &c. &c.

'Raritongo, Wankyfungo, Archipelago.' I protest this little woman read off each of these long words with an ease which perfectly astonished me. Many a lieutenant in her Majesty's Heavies would be puzzled with words half the length. Whitestock, by way of reward for her scholarship, gave her another pat on the head; having received which present with a curtsey, she went and put the book back into the window, and clambering back into the chair, resumed the hemming of the blue duster.

I suppose it was the smallness of these people, as well as their singular, neat, and tidy behaviour, which interested me so. Here were three creatures not so high as the table, with all the labours, duties, and cares of life upon their little shoulders, working and doing their duty like the biggest of my readers; regular, laborious, cheerful – content with small pittances, practising a hundred virtues of thrift and order.

Elizabeth, at ten years of age, might walk out of this house and take the command of a small establishment. She can wash, get up linen, cook, make purchases, and buy bargains. If I were ten years old and three feet in height, I would marry her, and we would go and live in a cupboard, and share the little half-pint pot for dinner. 'Melia, eight years of age, though inferior in accomplishments to her sister, is her equal in size, and can wash, scrub, hem, go errands, put her hand to the dinner, and make herself generally useful. In a word, she is fit to be a little housemaid, and to make everything but the beds, which she cannot as yet reach up to. As for Victoria's qualifications, they have been mentioned before. I wonder whether the Princess Alice can read off 'Raritongo,' &c. as glibly as this surprising little animal.

I asked the Curate's permission to make these young ladies a present, and accordingly produced the sum of sixpence to be divided amongst the three. 'What will you do with it?' I said, laying down the coin.

They answered, all three at once, in a little chorus, 'We'll give it to mother.' This verdict caused the disbursement of another sixpence, and it was explained to them that the sum was for their own private pleasures, and each was called upon to declare what she would purchase.

Elizabeth says, 'I would like twopenn'orth of meat, if you please, sir.'

'Melia: 'Ha'porth of treacle, three farthings' worth of milk, and the same of fresh bread.'

Victoria, speaking very quick, and gasping in an agitated manner: 'Ha'pny – aha – orange, and ha'pny – aha – apple, and ha'pny – aha – treacle, and – and –' here her imagination failed her. She did not know what to do with the rest of the money.

At this 'Melia actually interposed, 'Suppose she and Victoria subscribed a farthing apiece out of their money, so that Betsy might have a quarter of a pound of meat?' She added that her sister wanted it, and that it would do her good. Upon my word, she made the proposal and the calculations in an instant, and all of her own accord. And before we left them, Betsy had put on the queerest little black shawl and bonnet, and had a mug and a basket ready to receive the purchases in question.

Sedan Buildings has a particularly friendly look to me since that day. Peace be with you, O thrifty, kindly, simple, loving little maidens! May their voyage in life prosper! Think of the great journey before them, and the little cock-boat manned by babies venturing over the great stormy ocean.

II

Following the steps of little Betsy with her mug and basket, as she goes pattering down the street, we watch her into a grocer's shop, where a startling placard with 'DOWN AGAIN!' written on it announces that the Sugar Market is still in a depressed condition – and where she no doubt negotiates the purchase of a certain quantity of molasses. A little further on, in Lawfeldt Street, is Mr Filch's fine silversmith's shop, where a man may stand for a half hour and gaze with ravishment at the beautiful gilt cups and tankards, the stunning waistcoat chains, the little white cushions laid out with delightful diamond pins, gold horseshoes and splinter-bars, pearl owls, turquoise lizards and dragons, enamelled monkeys, and all sorts of agreeable monsters for your neckcloth. If I live to be a hundred, or if the girl of my heart were waiting for me at the corner of the Street, I never could pass Mr Filch's shop without having a couple of minutes' good stare at the window. I like to fancy myself dressed up in some of the jewellery. 'Spec, you rogue,' I say, 'suppose you were to get leave to wear three or four of those rings on your fingers; to stick that opal, round which twists a brilliant serpent with a ruby head, into your blue satin neckcloth; and to sport that gold jack-chain on your waistcoat. You might walk in the Park with that black whalebone prize-riding-whip, which has a head the size of a snuff box, surmounted with a silver jockey on a silver racehorse; and what a sensation you would create, if you took that large ram's horn with the cairngorm top out of your pocket, and offered a pinch of rappee to the company round!' A little attorney's clerk is staring in at the window, in whose mind very similar ideas are passing. What would he not give to wear that gold pin next Sunday in his blue hunting neckcloth? The ball of it is almost as big as those which are painted over the side door of Mr Filch's shop, which is down that passage which leads into Trotter's Court.

I have dined at a house where the silver dishes and covers came from Filch's, let out to their owner by Mr Filch for the day, and in charge of the grave-looking man whom I mistook for the butler. Butlers and ladies' maids innumerable have audiences of Mr Filch in his back parlour. There are suits of jewels which he and his shop have known for a half century past, so often have they been pawned to him. When we read in the *Court Journal* of Lady Fitzball's headdress of lappets and superb diamonds, it is because the jewels get a day rule from Filch's, and come back to his iron box as soon as the drawing-room is over. These jewels become historical among pawnbrokers. It was here that Lady Prigsby brought her diamonds one evening of last year, and desired hurriedly to raise two thousand pounds upon them, when Filch respectfully pointed out to her ladyship that she had pawned the stones already to his comrade, Mr Tubal, of Charing Cross. And, taking his hat, and putting the case under his arm, he went with her ladyship to the hack-cab in which she had driven to Lawfeldt Street, entered the vehicle with her, and they drove in silence to the back entrance of her mansion in Monmouth Square, where Mr Tubal's young man was still seated in the hall, waiting until her ladyship should be undressed.

We walked round the splendid shining shop and down the passage, which would be dark but that the gas-lit door is always swinging to and fro, as the people who come to pawn go in and out. You may be sure there is a gin-shop handy to all pawnbrokers.'

A lean man in a dingy dress is walking lazily up and down the flags of Trotter's Court. His ragged trousers trail in the slimy mud there. The doors of the pawnbroker's, and of the gin-shop on the other side, are banging to and fro: a little girl comes out of the former, with a tattered old handkerchief, and goes up and gives something to the dingy man. It is ninepence, just raised on his waistcoat. The man bids the child to 'cut away home', and when she is clear out of the court, he looks at us with a lurking scowl and walks into the gin-shop doors, which swing always opposite the pawnbroker's shop.

Why should he have sent the waistcoat wrapped in the ragged old cloth? Why should he have sent the child into that pawnbroker's box, and not have gone himself? He did not choose to let her see him to into the gin-shop – why drive her in at the opposite door? The child knows well enough whither he is gone. She might as well have carried an old waistcoat in her hand through the street as a ragged napkin. A sort of vanity, you see, drapes itself in that dirty rag; or is it a kind of debauched shame, which does not like to go naked? The fancy can follow the poor girl up the black alley, up the black stairs, into the bare room, where mother and children are starving, while the lazy ragamuffin, the family bully, is gone into the gin-shop to 'try our celebrated Cream of the Valley', as the bill in red letters bids him.

'I waited in this court the other day,' Whitestock said, 'just like that man, while a friend of mine went in to take her husband's tools out of pawn – an honest man – a journeyman shoemaker, who lives hard by.' And we went to call on the journeyman shoemaker – Randle's Buildings – two-pair back – over a blacking manufactory. The blacking was made by one manufacturer, who stood before a tub stirring up his produce, a good deal of which – and nothing else – was on the floor. We passed through this emporium, which abutted on a dank, steaming little court, and up the narrow stair to the two-pair back.

The shoemaker was at work with his recovered tools, and his wife was making woman's shoes (an inferior branch of the business) by him. A shrivelled child was lying on the bed in the corner of the room. There was no bedstead, and indeed scarcely any furniture, save the little table on which lay his tools and shoes – a fair-haired, lank, handsome young man, with a wife who may have been pretty once, in better times, and before starvation pulled her down. She had but one thin gown; it clung to a frightfully emaciated little body.

Their story was the old one. The man had been in good work, and had the fever. The clothes had been pawned, the furniture and bedstead had been sold, and they slept on the mattress; the mattress went, and they slept on the floor; the tools went, and the end of all things seemed at hand, when the gracious apparition of the Curate, with his umbrella, came and cheered those stricken-down poor folks.

The journeyman shoemaker must have been astonished at such a sight. He is not, or was not a church-goer. He is a man of 'advanced' opinions; believing that priests are hypocrites, and that clergymen in general drive about in coaches-and-four, and eat a tithe-pig a day. This proud priest got Mr Crispin a bed to lie upon, and some soup to eat; and (being the treasurer of certain good folks of his parish, whose charities he administers) as soon as the man was strong enough to work, the curate lent him money wherewith to redeem his tools, and which our friend is paying back by instalments at this day. And any man who has seen these two honest men talking together, would have said the shoemaker was the haughtier of the two.

We paid one more morning visit. This was with an order for work to a tailor of reduced circumstances and enlarged family. He had been a master, and was now forced to take work by the job. He who had commanded many men, was now fallen down to the ranks again. His wife told us all about his misfortunes. She is evidently very proud of them. 'He failed for seven thousand pounds,' the poor woman said, three or four times during the course of our visit. It gave her husband a sort of dignity to have been trusted for so much money.

The Curate must have heard that story many times, to which he now listened with great patience in the tailor's house – a large, clean, dreary, faint-looking room, smelling of poverty. Two little stunted, yellow-headed children, with lean pale faces and large protruding eyes, were at the window staring with all their might at Guy Fawkes, who was passing in the street, and making a great clattering and shouting outside, while the luckless tailor's wife was prating within about her husband's bygone riches. I shall not in a hurry forget the picture. The empty room in a dreary background; the tailor's wife in brown, stalking up and down the planks, talking endlessly; the solemn children staring out of the window as the sunshine fell on their faces, and honest Whitestock seated, listening, with the tails of his coat through the chair.

His business over with the tailor, we start again; Frank Whitestock trips through alley after alley, never getting any mud on his boots, somehow, and his white neckcloth making a wonderful shine in those shady places. He has all sorts of acquaintance, chiefly amongst the extreme youth, assembled at the doors or about the gutters. There was one small person occupied in emptying one of these rivulets with an oyster-shell, for the purpose, apparently, of making an aritifical lake in a hole hard by, whose solitary gravity and business air struck me much, while the Curate was very deep in conversation with a small coalman. A half-dozen of her comrades were congregated round a scraper and on a grating hard by, playing with a mangy little puppy, the property of the Curate's friend.

I know it is wrong to give large sums of money away promiscuously, but I could not help dropping a penny into the child's oyster-shell, as she came forward holding it before her like a tray. At first her expression was one rather of wonder than of pleasure at this influx of capital, and was certainly quite worth the small charge of one penny, at which it was purchased.

For a moment she did not seem to know what steps to take; but, having communed in her own mind, she presently resolved to turn them towards a neighbouring apple-stall, in the direction of which she went without a single word of compliment passing between us. Now, the children round the scraper were witnesses to the transaction. 'He's give her a penny,' one remarked to another, with hopes miserably disappointed that they might come in for a similar present.

She walked on to the apple-stall meanwhile, holding her penny behind her. And what did the other little ones do? They put down the puppy as if it had been so much dross. And one after another they followed the penny-piece to the apple-stall.

A DINNER IN THE CITY

I

O ut of a mere love of variety and contrast, I think we cannot do better, after leaving the wretched Whitestock among his starving parishioners, than transport ourselves to the City, where we are invited to dine with the Worshipful Company of Bellows-Menders, at their splendid Hall in Marrow-pudding Lane.

Next to eating good dinners, a healthy man with a benevolent turn of mind must like, I think, to read about them. When I was a boy, I had by heart the Barmecide's feast in the 'Arabian Nights'; and the culinary passages in Scott's novels (in which works there is a deal of good eating) always were my favourites. The Homeric poems are full, as everybody knows, of roast and boiled: and every year I look forward with pleasure to the newspapers of the 10th of November for the *menu* of the Lord Mayor's feast, which is sure to appear in those journals. What student of history is there who does not remember the City dinner given to the Allied Sovereigns in 1814? It is good even now, and to read it ought to make a man hungry, had he had five meals that day. In a word, I had long, long yearned in my secret heart to be present at a City festival. The last year's papers had a bill of fare commencing with 'four hundred tureens of turtle, each containing five pints'; and concluding with the pineapples and ices of the dessert. 'Fancy two thousand pints of turtle, my love,' I have often said to Mrs Spec, 'in a vast silver tank, smoking fragrantly, with lovely green islands of calipash and calipee floating about – why, my dear, if it had been invented in the time of Vitellius he would have bathed in it!'

'He would have been a nasty wretch,' Mrs Spec said, who thinks that cold mutton is the most wholesome food of man. However, when she heard what great company was to be present at the dinner, the Ministers of State, the Foreign Ambassadors, some of the bench of Bishops, no doubt the Judges, and a great portion of the Nobility, she was pleased at the card which was sent to her husband, and made a neat tie to my white neckcloth before I set off on the festive journey. She warned me to be very cautious, and obstinately refused to allow me the Chubb door key.

The very card of invitation is a curiosity. It is almost as big as a tea-tray. It gives one ideas of a vast, enormous hospitality. Gog and Magog in livery might leave it at your door. If a man is to eat up that card, heaven help us, I thought; the Doctor must be called in. Indeed, it was a Doctor who procured me the placard of invitation. Like all medical men who have published a book upon diet, Pilkington is a great gourmand, and he made a great favour of procuring the ticket for me from his brother of the Stock Exchange, who is a Citizen and a Bellows-Mender in his corporate capacity.

We drove in Pilkington's brougham to the place of *mangez-vous*, through the streets of the town, in the broad daylight, dressed out in our white waistcoats and ties; making a sensation upon all beholders by the premature splendour of our appearance. There is something grand in that hospitality of the citizens, who not only give you more to eat than other people, but who begin earlier than anybody else. Major Bangles, Captain Canterbury, and a host of the fashionables of my acquaintance, were taking their morning's ride in the Park as we drove through. You should have seen how they stared at us! It gave me a pleasure to be able to remark mentally, 'Look on, gents, we too are sometimes invited to the tables of the great.'

We fell in with numbers of carriages as we were approaching Citywards, in which reclined gentlemen with white neckcloths – grand equipages of foreign ambassadors, whose uniforms, and stars, and gold lace glistened within the carriages, while their servants with coloured cockades looked splendid without: these careered by the Doctor's brougham-horse, which was a little fatigued with his professional journeys in the morning. General Sir Roger Bluff, K.C.B., and

Colonel Tucker, were stepping into a cab at the United Service Club as we passed it. The veterans blazed in scarlet and gold lace. It seemed strange that men so famous, if they did not mount their chargers to go to dinner, should ride in any vehicle under a coach-and-six; and instead of having a triumphal car to conduct them to the City, should go thither in a rickety cab, driven by a ragged charioteer smoking a dhoodeen. In Cornhill we fell into a line, and formed a complete regiment of the aristocracy. Crowds were gathered round the steps of the old hall in Marrow-pudding Lane, and welcomed us nobility and gentry as we stepped out of our equipages at the door. The policemen could hardly restrain the ardour of these low fellows, and their sarcastic cheers were sometimes very unpleasant. There was one rascal who made an observation about the size of my white waistcoat, for which I should have liked to sacrifice him on the spot; but Pilkington hurried me, as the policemen did our little brougham, to give place to a prodigious fine equipage which followed, with immense grey horses, immense footmen in powder, and driven by a grave coachman in an episcopal wig.

A veteran officer in scarlet, with silver epaulets, and a profuse quantity of bullion and silver lace, descended from this carriage between the two footmen, and was nearly upset by his curling sabre, which had twisted itself between his legs, which were cased in duck trousers very tight, except about the knees (where they bagged quite freely), and with rich long white straps. I thought he must be a great man by the oddness of his uniform.

'Who is the General?' says I, as the old warrior, disentangling himself from his scimitar, entered the outer hall. 'Is it the Marquis of Anglesea, or the Rajah of Sarawak?'

I spoke in utter ignorance, as it appeared. 'That! Pooh,' says Pilkington; 'that is Mr Champignon, MP, of Whitehall Gardens and Fungus Abbey, Citizen and Bellows-Mender. His uniform is that of a Colonel of the Diddlesex Militia.' There was no end to similar mistakes on that day. A venerable man with a blue and gold uniform, and a large crimson sword-belt and brass-scabbarded sabre, passed presently, whom I mistook for a foreign ambassador at the least; whereas I found out that he was only a Billingsgate Commissioner – and a little

fellow in a blue livery, which fitted him so badly that I
thought he must be one of the hired waiters of the company,
who had been put into a coat that didn't belong to him, turned
out to be a real right honourable gent, who had been a
Minister once.

I was conducted upstairs by my friend to the gorgeous
drawing-room, where the company assembled, and where
there was a picture of George IV. I cannot make out what
public companies can want with a picture of George IV. A
fellow with a gold chain, and in a black suit, such as the
lamented Mr Cooper wore preparatory to execution in the last
act of *George Barnwell*, bawled out our names as we entered
the apartment. 'If my Eliza could hear that gentleman,'
thought I, 'roaring out the name of "Mr Spec!" in the presence
of at least two hundred Earls, Prelates, Judges, and distinguished characters!' It made little impression upon them,
however; and I slunk into the embrasure of a window, and
watched the company.

Every man who came into the room was, of course, ushered
in with a roar. 'His Excellency the Minister of Topinambo!'

the usher yelled; and the Minister appeared, bowing, and in tights. 'Mr Hoggin! The Right Honourable the Earl of Bareacres! Mr Snog! Mr Braddle! Mr Alderman Moodle! Mr Justice Bunker! Lieut-Gen. Sir Roger Bluff! Colonel Tucker! Mr Tims!' with the same emphasis and mark of admiration for us all as it were. The Warden of the Bellows-Menders came forward and made a profusion of bows to the various distinguished guests as they arrived. He, too, was in a court dress, with a sword and bag. His lady must like so to behold him turning out in arms and ruffles, shaking hands with Ministers, and bowing over his wine glass to their Excellencies the Foreign Ambassadors.

To be in a room with these great people gave me a thousand sensations of joy. Once, I am positive, the Secretary of the Tape and Sealing-Wax Office looked at me, and turning round to a noble lord in a red ribbon, evidently asked, 'Who is that?' Oh, Eliza, Eliza! How I wish you had been there! – or if not there, in the ladies' gallery in the dining hall, when the music began, and Mr Shadrach, Mr Meshech, and little Jack Oldboy (whom I recollect in the part of *Count Almaviva* any time these forty years), sang *Non nobis, Domine*.

But I am advancing matters prematurely. We are not in the grand dining hall as yet. The crowd grows thicker and thicker, so that you can't see people bow as they enter anymore. The usher in the gold chain roars out name after name: more ambassadors, more generals, more citizens, capitalists, bankers – among them Mr Rowdy, my banker, from whom I shrank guiltily from private financial reasons – and, last and greatest of all, 'The Right Honourable the Lord Mayor!'

That was a shock, such as I left on landing at Calais for the first time; on first seeing an Eastern bazaar: on first catching a sight of Mrs Spec; a new sensation, in a word. Till death I shall remember that surprise. I saw over the heads of the crowd, first a great sword borne up in the air: then a man in a fur cap of the shape of a flower pot; then I heard the voice shouting the august name – the crowd separated. A handsome man with a chain and gown stood before me. It was he. He? What do I say? It was his Lordship. I cared for nothing till dinner-time after that.

II

The glorious company of banqueteers were now pretty well all assembled; and I, for my part, attracted by an irresistible fascination, pushed nearer and nearer my Lord Mayor, and surveyed him, as the generals, lords, ambassadors, judges, and other bigwigs rallied round him as their centre, and, being introduced to his Lordship and each other, made themselves the most solemn and graceful bows; as if it had been the object of that general's life to meet that judge; and as if that Secretary of the Tape and Sealing-Wax Office, having achieved at length a presentation to the Lord Mayor, had gained the end of his existence, and might go home, singing a *Nunc dimittis*. Don Geronimo de Mulligan y Guayaba, Minister of the Republic of Topinambo (and originally descended from an illustrious Irish ancestor, who hewed out with his pickaxe in the Topinambo mines the steps by which his family have ascended to their present eminence), holding his cocked hat with the yellow cockade close over his embroidered coat-tails, conversed with Alderman Codshead, that celebrated Statesman, who was also in tights, with a sword and bag.

Of all the articles of the splendid court-dress of our aristocracy, I think it is those little bags which I admire most. The dear crisp curly little black darlings! They give a gentleman's back an indescribable grace and air of chivalry. They are at

151

once manly, elegant, and useful (being made of sticking-plaster, which can be applied afterwards to heal many a wound of domestic life). They are something extra appended to men, to enable them to appear in the presence of royalty. How vastly the idea of a Court increases in solemnity and grandeur when you think that a man cannot enter it without a tail!

These thoughts passed through my mind, and pleasingly diverted it from all sensations of hunger, while many friends around me were pulling out their watches, looking towards the great dining-room doors, rattling at the lock, (the door gasped open once or twice, and the nose of a functionary on the other side peeped in among us and entreated peace), and vowing it was scandalous, monstrous, shameful. If you ask an assembly of Englishmen to a feast, and accident or the cook delays it, they show their gratitude in this way. Before the supper rooms were thrown open at my friend Mrs Perkins's ball, I recollect Liversage at the door, swearing and growling as if he had met with an injury. So I thought the Bellows-Menders' guests seemed heaving into mutiny, when the great doors burst open in a flood of light, and we rushed, a black streaming crowd, into the gorgeous hall of banquet.

Every man sprang for his place with breathless rapidity. We knew where those places were beforehand; for a cunning map had been put into the hands of each of us by an officer of the Company, where every plate of this grand festival was numbered, and each gentleman's place was ticketed off. My wife keeps my card still in her album; and my dear eldest boy (who has a fine genius and appetite) will gaze on it for half an hour at a time, whereas he passes by the copies of verses and the flower-pieces with an entire indifference.

The vast hall flames with gas, and is emblazoned all over with the arms of bygone Bellows-Menders. August portraits decorate the walls. The Duke of Kent in scarlet, with a crooked sabre, stared me firmly in the face during the whole entertainment. The Duke of Cumberland, in a hussar uniform, was at my back, and I knew was looking down into my plate. The eyes of those gaunt portraits follow you everywhere. The Prince Regent has been mentioned before. He has his place of honour over the Great Bellows-Menders' chair, and surveys the high table glittering with plate, épergnes, candles, hock-glasses, moulds of blancmange stuck over with flowers, gold statues holding up baskets of barley sugar, and a thousand objects of art. Piles of immense gold cans and salvers rose up in buffets behind this high table; towards which presently, and in a grand procession – the band in the gallery overhead blowing out the Bellows-Menders' march – a score of City tradesmen and their famous guests walked solemnly between our rows of tables.

Grace was said, not by the professional devotees who sang 'Non Nobis' at the end of the meal, but by a chaplain somewhere in the room, and the turtle began. Armies of waiters came rushing in with tureens of this broth of the City.

There was a gentleman near us – a very lean old Bellows-

Mender indeed, who had three platefuls. His old hands trembled, and his plate quivered with excitement, as he asked again and again. That old man is not destined to eat much more of the green fat of this life. As he took it, he shook all over like the jelly in the dish opposite to him. He gasped out a quick laugh once or twice to his neighbour, when his two or three old tusks showed, still standing up in those jaws which had swallowed such a deal of calipash. He winked at the waiters, knowing them from former banquets.

This banquet, which I am describing at Christmas, took place at the end of May. At that time the vegetables called pease were exceedingly scarce, and cost six-and-twenty shillings a quart.

'There are two hundred quarts of pease', said the old fellow, winking with blood-shot eyes, and a laugh that was perfectly frightful. They were consumed with the fragrant ducks, by those who were inclined: or with the venison, which now came in.

That was a great sight. On a centre table in the hall, on which already stood a cold baron of beef – a grotesque piece of meat – a dish as big as a dish in a pantomime, with a little Standard of England stuck into the top of it, as if it were round this we were to rally – on this centre table, six men placed as many huge dishes under cover; and at a given signal the master cook and five assistants in white caps and jackets marched rapidly up to the dish covers, which being withdrawn, discovered to our sight six haunches, on which the six carvers, taking out six sharp knives from their girdles, began operating.

It was, I say, like something out of a Gothic romance, or a grotesque fairy pantomime. Feudal barons must have dined so five hundred years ago. One of those knives may have been the identical blade which Walworth plunged into Wat Tyler's ribs, and which was afterwards caught up into the City Arms, where it blazes. (Not that any man can seriously believe that Wat Tyler was hurt by the dig of the jolly old Mayor in the red gown and chain, any more than that pantaloon is singed by the great poker, which is always forthcoming at the present season.) Here we were practising the noble custom of the good old times, imitating our glorious forefathers, rallying round our old institutions, like true Britons. These very flagons and platters were in the room before us, ten times as big as any we use or want nowadays. They served us a grace-cup as large as a plate-basket, and at the end they passed us a rosewater dish, into which Pepys might have dipped his napkin. Pepys? – what do I say? Richard III, Coeur-de-Lion, Guy of Warwick, Gog and Magog. I don't know how antique the articles are.

Conversation, rapid and befitting the place and occasion, went on all round. 'Waiter, where's the turtle-fins?' – Gobble, gobble. 'Nice Punch or My deary, sir?' 'Smelts or salmon, Jowler my boy?' 'Always take cold beef after turtle.' – Hobble-gobble. 'This year pease have no taste.' Hobble-gobbleobble. 'Jones, a glass of 'Ock with you? Smith, jine us? Waiter, three 'Ocks. S, mind your manners! There's Mrs S a-looking at you from the gallery.' – Hobble-obbl-gobble-gob-gob-gob. A steam of meats, a flare of candles, a rushing to and fro of waiters, a ceaseless clinking of glass and steel, a dizzy mist of gluttony, out of which I see my old friend of the turtle-soup making terrific play among the pease, his knife darting down his throat.

* * * * *

It is all over. We can eat no more. We are full of Bacchus and fat venison. We lay down our weapons and rest. 'Why, in the name of goodness,' says I, turning round to Pilkington, who had behaved at dinner like a doctor; 'why —?'

But a great rap, tap, tap proclaimed grace, after which the professional gentlemen sang out, '*Non Nobis*', and then the dessert and the speeches began; about which we shall speak in the third course of our entertainment.

III

n the hammer having ceased its tapping, Mr Chisel, the immortal toastmaster, who presided over the President, roared out to my three professional friends, 'Non Nobis'; and what is called 'the business of the evening' commenced.

First, the Warden of the Worshipful Society of the Bellows-Menders proposed 'Her Majesty' in a reverential voice. We all stood up respectfully, Chisel yelling out to us to 'Charge our glasses'. The royal health having been imbibed, the professional gentlemen ejaculated a part of the National Anthem; and I do not mean any disrespect to them personally, in mentioning that this eminently religious hymn was performed by Messrs. Shadrach and Meschech, two well-known melodists of the Hebrew persuasion. We clinked our glasses at the conclusion of the anthem, making more dents upon the time-worn old board, where many a man present had clinked for George III, clapped for George IV, rapped for William IV, and was rejoiced to bump the bottom of his glass as a token of reverence for our present Sovereign.

Here, as in the case of the Hebrew melophonists, I would insinuate no wrong thought. Gentlemen, no doubt, have the loyal emotions which exhibit themselves by clapping glasses on the tables. We do it at home. Let us make no doubt that the bellows-menders, tailors, authors, public characters, judges, aldermen, sheriffs, and what not, shout out a health for the Sovereign every night at their banquets, and that their families fill round and drink the same toast from the bottles of half-guinea Burgundy.

'His Royal Highness Prince Albert, and Albert Prince of Wales, and the rest of the Royal Family,' followed, Chisel yelling out the august titles, and all of us banging away with our glasses, as if we were seriously interested in drinking healths to this royal race: as if drinking healths could do anybody any good; as if the imprecations of a company of bellows-menders, aldermen, magistrates, tailors, authors, tradesmen, ambassadors, who did not care a twopenny-piece for all the royal families in Europe, could somehow affect heaven kindly towards their Royal Highnesses by their tipsy vows, under the presidence of Mr Chisel.

The Queen Dowager's health was next prayed for by us Bacchanalians, I need not say with what fervency and efficacy. This prayer was no sooner put up by the Chairman, with Chisel as his Boanerges of a Clerk, than the elderly Hebrew gentlemen before mentioned began striking up a wild patriotic ditty about the 'Queen of the Isles, on whose sea-grit shores the bright sun smiles, and the ocean roars; whose cliffs never knew, since the bright sun rose, but a people true, who scorned all foes. Oh, a people true, who scorn all wiles, inhabit you, bright Queen of the Isles. Bright Queen – Bright Quee-ee-ee-ee-ee-en awf the Isles!' or words to that effect, which Shadrach took up and warbled across his glass to Meshech, which Meshech trolled away to his brother singer, until the ditty was ended, nobody understanding a word of what it meant; not Oldboy – not the old or young Israelite minstrel his companion – not we, who were clinking our glasses – not Chisel, who was urging us and the Chairman on – not the Chairman and the guests in embroidery – not the kind, exalted, and amiable lady whose health we were making believe to drink, certainly, and in order to render whose name welcome to the Powers of whom we recommended her safety, we offered up, through the mouths of three singers, hired for the purpose, a perfectly insane and irrelevant song.

'Why,' says I to Pilkington, 'the Chairman and the grand guests might just as well get up and dance round the table, or cut off Chisel's head and pop it into a turtle-soup tureen, or go through any other mad ceremony as the last. Which of us here cares for her Majesty the Queen Dowager, any more than for a virtuous and eminent lady, whose goodness and private worth appear in all her acts? What the deuce has that absurd song about the Queen of the Isles to do with her Majesty, and how does it set us all stamping with our glasses on the mahogany?' Chisel bellowed out another toast – 'The Army'; and we were silent in admiration, while Sir George Bluff, the greatest General present, rose to return thanks.

Our end of the table was far removed from the thick of the affair, and we only heard, as it were, the indistinct cannonading of the General, whose force had just advanced into action. We saw an old gentleman with white whiskers, and a flaring scarlet coat covered with stars and gilding, rise up with a frightened and desperate look, and declare that 'this was the proudest – a-hem – moment of his – a-hem – unworthy as he was – a-hem – as a member of the British – a-hem – who had fought under the illustrious Duke of – a-hem – his joy was to come among the Bellows-Menders – a-hem – and inform the great merchants of the greatest City of the – hum – that a British – a-hem – was always ready to do his – hum. Napoleon – Salamanca – a-hem – had witnessed their – hum, haw – and should any other – hum – ho – casion which he deeply deprecated – haw – there were men now around him – a-haw – who, inspired by the Bellows-Menders' Company and the City of London – a-hum – would do their duty as – a-hum – a-haw – a-hah.' Immense cheers, yells, hurrays, roars, glass-smackings, and applause followed this harangue, at the end of which the three Israelites, encouraged by Chisel, began a military cantata – 'Oh, the sword and shield – on the battlefield – Are the joys that best we love, boys – Where the Grenadiers, with their pikes and spears, through the ranks of the foemen shove, boys – Where the bold hurray, strikes dread dismay, in the ranks of the dead and dyin' – and the baynet clanks in the Frenchmen's ranks, as they fly from the British Lion.' (I repeat, as before, that I quote from memory.)

Then the Secretary of the Tape and Sealing-Wax Office rose to return thanks for the blessings which we begged upon the Ministry. He was, he said, but a humble – the humblest member of that body. The suffrages which that body had received from the nation were gratifying, but the most gratifying testimonial of all was the approval of the Bellows-

Menders' Company. (*Immense applause.*) Yes, among the most enlightened of the mighty corporations of the City, the most enlightened was the Bellows-Menders'. Yes, he might say, in consonance with their motto, and in defiance of illiberality, *Afflavit veritas et dissipati sunt.* (*Enormous applause.*) Yes, the thanks and pride that were boiling with emotion in his bosom, trembled to find utterance at his lip. Yes, the proudest moment of his life, the crown of his ambition, the meed of his early hopes and struggles and aspirations, was at that moment won in the approbation of the Bellows-Menders. Yes, his children should know that he too had attended at those great, those noble, those joyous, those ancient festivals, and that he too, the humble individual who from his heart pledged the assembled company in a bumper – that he too was a Bellows-Mender.

Shadrach, Meshech, and Oldboy, at this began singing, I don't know for what reason, a rustic madrigal, describing, 'Oh, the joys of bonny May – bonny May – a-a-ay, when the birds sing on the spray,' &c., which never, as I could see, had the least relation to that or any other Ministry, but which was, nevertheless, applauded by all present. And then the Judges returned thanks; and the Clergy returned thanks; and the Foreign Ministers had an innings (all interspersed by my friends' indefatigable melodies); and the distinguished foreigners present, especially Mr Washington Jackson, were greeted, and that distinguished American rose amidst thunders of applause.

He explained how Broadway and Cornhill were in fact the same. He showed how Washington was in fact an Englishman, and how Franklin would never have been an American but for his education as a printer in Lincoln's Inn Fields. He declared that Milton was his cousin, Locke his ancestor, Newton his dearest friend, Shakespeare his grandfather, or more or less – he vowed that he had wept tears of briny anguish on the pedestal of Charing Cross – kissed with honest fervour the clay of Runnymede – that Ben Jonson and Samuel – that Pope and Dryden, and Dr Watts and Swift were the darlings of *his* hearth and home, as of ours, and in a speech of about five-and-thirty minutes, explained to us a series of complimentary sensations very hard to repeat or to remember.

But I observed that, during his oration, the gentlemen who report for the daily papers were occupied with their wine instead of their notebooks – that the three singers of Israel yawned and showed many signs of disquiet and inebriety, and that my old friend, who had swallowed the three plates of turtle, was sound asleep.

Pilkington and I quitted the banqueting hall, and went into the tea-room, where gents were assembled still, drinking slops and eating buttered muffins, until the grease trickled down their faces. Then I resumed the query which I was just about to put, when grace was called, and the last chapter ended. 'And, gracious goodness!' I said, 'what can be the meaning of a ceremony so costly, so uncomfortable, so unsavoury, so unwholesome as this? Who is called upon to pay two or three guineas for my dinner now, in this blessed year 1847? Who is it that *can* want muffins after such a banquet? Are there no poor? Is there no reason? Is this monstrous belly-worship to exist for ever?'

'Spec,' the Doctor said, 'you had best come away. I make no doubt that you for one have had too much.' And we went to his brougham. May nobody have such a headache on this happy New Year as befell the present writer on the morning after the Dinner in the City!

WAITING AT THE STATION

e are amongst a number of people waiting for the Blackwall train at the Fenchurch Street Station. Some of us are going a little farther than Blackwall – as far as Gravesend; some of us are going even farther than Gravesend – to Port Phillip in Australia, leaving behind the *patrice fines* and the pleasant fields of Old England. It is rather a queer sensation to be in the same boat and station with a party that is going upon so prodigious a journey. One speculates about them with more than an ordinary interest, thinking of the difference between your fate and theirs, and that we shall never behold these faces again.

Some eight-and-thirty women are sitting in the large Hall of the station, with bundles, baskets, and light baggage, waiting for the steamer, and the orders to embark. A few friends are taking leave of them, bonnets are laid together, and whispering going on. A little crying is taking place; – only a very little crying, – and among those who remain, as it seems to me, not those who are going away. They leave behind them little to weep for; they are going from bitter cold and hunger, constant want and unavailing labour. Why should they be sorry to quit

161

a mother who has been so hard to them as our country has been? How many of these women will ever see the shore again, upon the brink of which they stand, and from which they will depart in a few minutes more? It makes one sad and ashamed too, that they should not be more sorry. But how are you to expect love where you have given such scanty kindness? If you saw your children glad at the thoughts of leaving you, and for ever: would you blame yourselves or them? It is not that the children are ungrateful, but the home was unhappy, and the parents indifferent or unkind. You are in the wrong, under whose government they only had neglect and wretchedness; not they, who can't be called upon to love such an unlovely thing as misery, or to make any other return for neglect but indifference and aversion.

You and I, let us suppose again, are civilized persons. We have been decently educated: and live decently every day, and wear tolerable clothes, and practise cleanliness: and love the arts and graces of life. As we walk down this rank of eight-and-thirty female emigrants, let us fancy that we are at Melbourne, and not in London, and that we have come down from our sheep-walks, or clearings, having heard of the arrival of forty honest, well-recommended young women, and having a natural longing to take a wife home to the bush – which of these would you like? If you were an Australian Sultan, to which of these would you throw the handkerchief? I am afraid not one of them. I fear, in our present mood of mind, we should mount horse and return to the country, preferring a solitude, and to be a bachelor, than to put up with one of these for a companion. There is no girl here to tempt you by her looks: (and, world-wiseacre as you are, it is by these you are principally moved) – there is no pretty, modest, red-cheeked rustic, – no neat, trim little grisette, such as what we call a gentleman might cast his eyes upon without too much derogating, and might find favour in the eyes of a man about town. No; it is a homely bevy of women with scarcely any beauty amongst them – their clothes are decent, but not the least picturesque – their faces are pale and care-worn for the most part – how, indeed, should it be otherwise, seeing that they have known care and want all their days? – there they sit, upon bare benches, with dingy bundles, and great cotton umbrellas – and the truth is, you are not a hardy colonist, a feeder of sheep, feller of trees, a hunter of kangaroos – but a London man, and my lord the Sultan's cambric handkerchief is scented with Bond Street perfumery – you put it in your pocket, and couldn't give it to any one of these women.

They are not like you, indeed. They have not your tastes and feelings: your education and refinements. They would not understand a hundred things which seem perfectly simple to you. They would shock you a hundred times a day by as many deficiencies of politeness, or by outrages upon the Queen's English – by practices entirely harmless, and yet in your eyes actually worse than crimes – they have large hard hands and clumsy feet. The woman you love must have pretty soft fingers that you may hold in yours: must speak her language properly, and at least when you offer her your heart, must return hers with its *h* in the right place, as she whispers that it is yours, or you will have none of it. If she says, 'O Hedward, I ham so unappy to think I shall never beold you agin,' – though her emotion on leaving you might be perfectly tender and genuine, you would be obliged to laugh. If she said, 'Hedward, my art is yours for hever and hever' (and anybody heard her), she might as well stab you, – you couldn't accept the most faithful affection offered in such terms – you are a town-bred man, I say, and your handkerchief smells of Bond Street musk and millefleur. A sun-burnt settler out of the Bush won't feel any of these exquisite tortures: or understand this kind of laughter: or object to Molly because her hands are coarse and her ankles thick: but he will take her back to his farm, where she will nurse his children, bake his dough, milk his cows, and cook his kangaroo for him.

But between you, an educated Londoner, and that woman, is not the union absurd and impossible? Would it not be unbearable for either? Solitude would be incomparably pleasanter than such a companion. – You might take her with a handsome fortune, perhaps, were you starving; but then it is because you want a house and carriage, let us say (*your* necessaries of life), and must have them even if you purchase them with your precious person. You do as much, or your sister does as much, every day. That, however, is not the point: I am not talking about the meanness to which your worship may be possibly obliged to stoop, in order, as you say, 'to keep up your rank in society' – only stating that this immense social difference does exist. You don't like to own it: or don't choose to talk about it, and such things had much better not be spoken about at all. I hear your worship say, there must be differences in rank and so forth! Well! out with it at once: you don't think Molly is your equal – nor indeed is she in the possession of many artificial acquirements. She can't make Latin verses, for example, as you used to do at school; she can't speak French and Italian, as your wife very likely can, &c. – and in so far she is your inferior, and your amiable lady's.

But what I note, what I marvel at, what I acknowledge, what I am ashamed of, what is contrary to Christian morals, manly modesty and honesty, and to the national well-being, is that there should be that immense social distinction between the well-dressed classes (as, if you will permit me, we will call ourselves), and our brethren and sisters in the fustian jackets and pattens. If you deny it for your part, I say that you are mistaken, and deceive yourself woefully. I say that you have been educated to it through Gothic ages, and have had it handed down to you from your fathers (not that they were anybody in particular, but respectable, well-dressed progenitors, let us say for a generation or two) – from your well-dressed fathers before you. How long ago is it that our preachers were teaching the poor 'to know their station?' that it was the peculiar boast of Englishmen, that any man, the humblest among us, could, by talent, industry, and good luck, hope to take his place in the aristocracy of his country, and that we pointed with pride to Lord This, who was the grandson of a barber; and to Earl That, whose father was an apothecary? What a multitude of most respectable folks pride themselves on these things still! The gulf is not impassable, because one man in a million swims over it, and we hail him for his strengh and success. He has landed on the happy island. He is one of the aristocracy. Let us clap hands and applaud. There's no country like ours for rational freedom.

If you go up and speak to one of these women, as you do, (and very good-naturedly, and you can't help that confounded condescension), she curtsies and holds down her head meekly, and replies with modesty, as becomes her station, to your honour with the clean shirt and the well-made coat. 'And so she should', is what hundreds of thousands of us, rich and poor, say still. Both believe this to be bounden duty; and that a poor person should naturally bob her head to a rich one physically and morally.

Let us get her last curtsey from her as she stands here upon the English shore. When she gets into the Australian woods her back won't bend except to her labour; or, if it do, from old habit and the reminiscence of the old country, do you suppose her children will be like that timid creature before you? They will know nothing of that Gothic society, with its ranks and hierarchies, its cumbrous ceremonies, its glittering antique paraphernalia, in which we have been educated; in which rich and poor still acquiesce, and which multitudes of both still admire: far removed from these old-world traditions, they will be bred up in the midst of plenty, freedom, manly brotherhood. Do you think if your worship's grandson goes into the Australian woods, or meets the grandchild of one of yonder women by the banks of the Warrawarra, the Australian will take a hat off or bob a curtsey to the new comer? He will hold out his hand, and say, 'Stranger, come into my house and take a shakedown, and have a share of our supper. You come out of the old country, do you? There was some people were kind to my grandmother there, and sent her out to Melbourne. Times are changed since then – come in and welcome!'

What a confession it is that we have almost all of us been obliged to make! A clever and earnest-minded writer gets a commission from the *Morning Chronicle* newspaper, and reports upon the state of our poor in London; he goes amongst labouring people and poor of all kinds – and brings back what? A picture of human life so wonderful, so awful, so piteous and pathetic, so exciting and terrible, that readers of romances own they never read anything like it; and that the griefs, struggles, strange adventures here depicted, exceed anything that any of us could imagine. Yes; and these wonders and terrors have been lying by your door and mine ever since we had a door of our own. We had but to go a hundred yards off and see for ourselves, but we never did. Don't we pay poor-rates, and are they not heavy enough in the name of patience? Very true; and we have our own private pensioners, and give away some of our superfluity, very likely. You are not unkind; not ungenerous. But of such wondrous and complicated misery as this you confess you had no idea. No. How should you? – you and I – we are of the upper classes; we have had hitherto no community with the poor. We never speak a word to the servant who waits on us for twenty years; we condescend to employ a tradesman, keeping him at a proper distance, mind, of course, at a proper distance – we laugh at his young men, if they dance, jig, and amuse themselves like their betters, and call them counter-jumpers, snobs, and what not; of his workmen we know nothing, how pitilessly they are ground down, how they live and die, here close by us at the backs of our houses; until some poet like Hood wakes and sings that dreadful 'Song of the Shirt'; some prophet like Carlyle rises up and denounces woe; some clear-sighted, energetic man like the writer of the Chronicle travels into the poor man's country for us, and comes back with his tale of terror and wonder.

Awful, awful poor man's country! The bell rings, and these eight-and-thirty women bid adieu to it, rescued from it (as a few thousands more will be) by some kind people who are interested on their behalf. In two hours more, the steamer lies alongside the ship Culloden, which will bear them to their new home. Here are the berths aft for the unmarried women, the married couples are in the midships, the bachelors in the fore-part of the ship. Above and below decks it swarms and echoes with the bustle of departure. The Emigration Commissioner comes and calls over their names; there are old and young, large families, numbers of children already accustomed to the ship, and looking about with amused unconsciousness. One was born but just now on board; he will not know how to speak English till he is fifteen thousand miles away from home. Some of these kind people whose bounty and benevolence organized the Female Emigration Scheme, are here to give a last word and shake of the hand to their protégées. They hang sadly and gratefully round their patrons. One of them, a clergyman, who has devoted himself to his good work, says a few words to them at parting. It is a solemn minute indeed – for those who (with the few thousands who will follow them) are leaving the country and escaping from the question between rich and poor; and what for those who remain? But, at least, those who go will remember that in their misery here they found gentle hearts to love and pity them, and generous hands to give them succour, and will plant in the new country this grateful tradition of the old. – May heaven's good mercy speed them!

A NIGHT'S PLEASURE

I

aving made a solemn engagement during the last mid-summer holidays with my young friend Augustus Jones, that we should go to a Christmas Pantomime together, and being accommodated by the obliging proprietors of Covent Garden Theatre with a private box for last Tuesday, I invited not only him, but some other young friends to be present at the entertainment. The two Miss Twiggs, the charming daughters of the Rev Mr Twigg, our neighbour; Miss Minny Twigg, their youngest sister, eight years of age; and their maternal aunt, Mrs Captain Flather, as the chaperon of the young ladies, were the four other partakers of this amusement with myself and Mr Jones.

It was agreed that the ladies, who live in Montpellier Square, Brompton, should take up myself and Master Augustus at the 'Sarcophagus Club', which is on the way to the theatre, and where we two gentlemen dined on the day appointed. Cox's most roomy fly, the mouldy green one, in which he insists on putting the roaring grey horse, was engaged for the happy evening. Only an intoxicated driver (as Cox's man always is) could ever, I am sure, get that animal into a trot. But the utmost fury of the whip will not drive him into a dangerous pace; and besides, the ladies were protected by Thomas, Mrs Flather's page, a young man with a gold band to his hat, and a large gilt knob on the top, who ensured the safety of the cargo, and really gave the vehicle the dignity of one's own carriage.

The dinner-hour at the 'Sarcophagus' being appointed for five o'clock, and a table secured in the strangers' room, Master Jones was good enough to arrive (under the guardianship of the Colonel's footman) about half an hour before the appointed time, and the interval was by him partly passed in conversation, but chiefly in looking at a large silver watch which he possesses, and in hoping that we shouldn't be late.

I made every attempt to pacify and amuse my young guest, whose anxiety was not about the dinner but about the play. I tried him with a few questions about Greek and Mathematics – a sort of talk, however, which I was obliged speedily to abandon, for I found he knew a great deal more upon these subjects than I did – (it is disgusting how preternaturally learned the boys of our day are, by the way). I engaged him to relate anecdotes about his schoolfellows and ushers, which he did, but still in a hurried, agitated, nervous manner – evidently thinking about that sole absorbing subject, the pantomime.

A neat little dinner, served in Botibol's best manner (our *chef* at the 'Sarcophagus' knows when he has to deal with a connoisseur, and would as soon serve me up his own ears as a *réchauffé* dish), made scarcely any impression on young Jones. After a couple of spoonfuls, he pushed away the Palestine soup, and took out his large silver watch – he applied two or three times to the chronometer during the fish period – and it was not until I had him employed upon an omelette, full of apricot jam, that the young gentleman was decently tranquil.

With the last mouthful of the omelette he began to fidget again; and it still wanted a quarter of an hour to six. Nuts, almonds and raisins, figs (the almost never-failing soother of youth), I hoped might keep him quiet, and laid before him all those delicacies. But he beat the devil's tattoo with the nut crackers, had out the watch time after time, declared that it stopped, and made such a ceaseless kicking on the legs of his chair, that there were moments when I wished he was back in the parlour with Mrs Jones, his mamma.

I know oldsters who have a savage pleasure in making boys drunk – a horrid thought of this kind may, perhaps, have crossed my mind. 'If I could get him to drink half a dozen glasses of that heavy port, it might soothe him and make him sleep', I may have thought. But he would only take a couple glasses of wine. He said he didn't like more; that his father did not wish him to take more: and abashed by his frank and honest demeanour, I would not press him, of course, a single moment further, and so was forced to take the bottle to myself, to soothe me instead of my young guest.

He was almost frantic at a quarter to seven, by which time the ladies had agreed to call for us, and for about five minutes was perfectly dangerous. 'We shall be late, I know we shall; I said we should! I am sure it's seven, past, and that the box will be taken!' and countless other exclamations of fear and impatience passed through his mind. At length we heard a carriage stop, and a Club servant entering and directing himself towards our table. Young Jones did not wait to hear him speak, but cried out, – 'Hooray, here they are!' flung his napkin over his head, dashed off his chair, sprang at his hat like a kitten at a ball, and bounced out of the door, crying out, 'Come along, Mr Spec!' whilst the individual addressed much more deliberately followed. 'Happy Augustus!' I mentally exclaimed. 'O thou brisk and bounding votary of pleasure! When the virile toga has taken the place of the jacket and turned-down collar, that *Columbine*, who will float before you a goddess tonight, will only be a third-rate dancing female, with rouge and large feet. You will see the ropes by which the genii come down, and the dirty crumpled knees of the fairies – and you won't be in such a hurry to leave a good bottle of port as now at the pleasant age of thirteen.' – [By the way, boys are made so abominably comfortable and odiously happy, nowadays, that when I look back to 1802, and my own youth, I get in a rage with the whole race of boys, and feel inclined to flog them all round.] Paying the bill, I say, and making these leisurely observations, I passed under the hall of the 'Sarcophagus', where Thomas, the page, touched the gold-knobbed hat respectfully to me, in a manner which I think must have rather surprised old General Growler, who was unrolling himself of his muffetees and wrappers, and issued into the street, where Cox's fly was in waiting: the windows up, and whitened with a slight frost: the silhouettes of the dear beings within dimly visible against the chemists' light opposite the Club; and Master Augustus already kicking his heels on the box, by the side of the inebriated driver.

I caused the youth to descend from that perch, and the door of the fly being opened, thrust him in. Mrs Captain Flather, of course, occupied the place of honour – an uncommonly capacious woman, – and one of the young ladies made a retreat from the front seat, in order to leave it vacant for myself; but I insisted on not incommoding Mrs Captain F, and that the two darling children should sit beside her, while I occupied the place of back bodkin between the two Miss Twiggs.

They were attired in white, covered up with shawls, with bouquets in their laps, and their hair dressed evidently for the occasion: Mrs Flather in her red velvet of course, with her large gilt state turban.

She saw that we were squeezed on our side of the carriage, and made an offer to receive me on hers.

Squeezed? I should think we *were*; but, O Emily, O Louisa, you mischievous little black-eyed creatures, who would dislike being squeezed by you? I wished it was to York we were going, and not to Covent Garden. How swiftly the moments passed. We were at the playhouse in no time: and Augustus plunged instantly out of the fly over the shins of everybody.

A NIGHT'S PLEASURE

II

e took possession of the private box assigned to us: and Mrs Flather seated herself in the place of honour – each of the young ladies taking it by turns to occupy the other corner. Miss Minny and Master Jones occupied the middle places; and it was pleasant to watch the young gentleman throughout the performance of the comedy – during which he was never quiet for two minutes – now shifting his chair, now swinging to and fro upon it, now digging his elbows into the capacious sides of Mrs Captain Flather, now beating with his boots against the front of the box, or trampling upon the skirts of Mrs Flather's velvet garment.

He occupied himself unceasingly, too, in working up and down Mrs F's double-barrelled French opera-glass – not a little to the detriment of that instrument and the wrath of the owner; indeed I have no doubt, that had not Mrs Flather reflected that Mrs Colonel Jones gave some of the most elegant parties in London, to which she was very anxious to be invited, she would have boxed Master Augustus's ears in the presence of the whole audience of Covent Garden.

One of the young ladies was, of course, obliged to remain in the back row with Mr Spec. We could not see much of the play over Mrs F's turban; but I trust that we were not unhappy in our retired position. O Miss Emily! O Miss Louisa! there is one who would be happy to sit for a week close by either of you, though it were on one of those abominable little private-box chairs. I know, for my part, that every time the box-keeperess popped in her head, and asked if we would take any refreshment, I thought the interruption odious.

Our young ladies, and their stout chaperone and aunt, had come provided with neat little bouquets of flowers, in which they evidently took a considerable pride, and which were laid, on their first entrance, on the ledge in front of our box.

But, presently, on the opposite side of the house, Mrs Cutbush, of Pocklington Gardens, appeared with her daughters, and bowed in a patronizing manner to the ladies of our party, with whom the Cutbush family had a slight acquaintance.

Before ten minutes, the bouquests of our party were whisked away from the ledge of the box. Mrs Flather dropped hers to the ground, where Master Jones's feet speedily finished it; Miss Louisa Twigg let hers fall into her lap, and covered it with her pocket-handkerchief. Uneasy signals passed between her and her sister. I could not, at first, understand what event had occurred to make these ladies so unhappy.

At last the secret came out. The Misses Cutbush had bouquets like little haystacks before them. Our small nosegays, which had quite satisfied the girls until now, had become odious in their little jealous eyes; and the Cutbushes triumphed over them.

I have joked the ladies subsequently on this adventure; but not one of them will acknowledge the charge against them. It was mere accident that made them drop the flowers – pure accident. *They* jealous of the Cutbushes – not they, indeed; and of course, each person on his head is welcome to his own opinion.

How different, meanwhile, was the behaviour of my young friend Master Jones, who is not as yet sophisticated by the world. He not only nodded to his father's servant, who had taken a place in the pit, and was to escort his young master home, but he discovered a schoolfellow in the pit likewise. 'By Jove, there's Smith!' he cried out, as if the sight of Smith was the

most extraordinary event in the world. He pointed out Smith
to all of us. He never ceased nodding, winking, grinning,
telegraphing, until he had succeeded in attracting the attention
not only of Master Smith, but of the greater part of the house;
and whenever anything in the play struck him as worthy of
applause, he instantly made signals to Smith below, and
shook his fist at him, as much as to say, 'By Jove, old fellow,
ain't it good? I say, Smith, isn't it *prime*, old boy?' He actually
made remarks on his fingers to Master Smith during the
performance.

I confess he was one of the best parts of the night's
entertainment, to me. How Jones and Smith will talk about
the play when they meet after holidays! And not only then will
they remember it, but all their lives long. Why do you
remember that play you saw thirty years ago, and forget the
one over which you yawned last week? 'Ah, my brave little
boy,' I thought in my heart, 'twenty years hence you will
recollect this, and have forgotten many a better thing. You
will have been in love twice or thrice by that time, and have
forgotten it; you will have buried your wife and forgotten her;
you will have had ever so many friendships and forgotten
them. You and Smith won't care for each other, very probably; but you'll remember all the actors and the plot of this
piece we are seeing.'

I protest I have forgotten it myself. In our back row we
could not see or hear much of the performance (and no great
loss) – fitful bursts of elocution only occasionally reaching us,
in which we could recognize the well-known nasal twang of
the excellent Mr Stupor, who peformed the part of the young
hero; or the ringing laughter of Mrs Belmore, who had to
giggle through the whole piece.

It was one of Mr Boyster's comedies of English life. Frank
Nightrake (Stupor) and his friend Bob Fitzoffley appeared in
the first scene, having a conversation with that impossible
valet of English Comedy, whom any gentleman would turn
out of doors before he could get through half a length of the
dialogue assigned. I caught only a glimpse of this act. Bob,
like a fashionable young dog of the aristocracy (the character
was played by Bulger, a meritorious man, but very stout, and
nearly fifty years of age), was dressed in a rhubarb-coloured

bodycoat with brass buttons, a couple of under-waistcoats, a blue satin stock with a paste brooch in it, and an eighteenpenny cane, which he never let out of his hand, and with which he poked fun at everybody. Frank Nightrake, on the contrary, being at home, was attired in a very close-fitting chintz dressing-gown, lined with glazed red calico, and was seated before a large pewter teapot, at breakfast. And, as your true English Comedy is the representation of nature, I could not but think how little these figures on the stage, and the dialogue which they used, were to the appearance and talk of English gentlemen of the present day.

The dialogue went on somewhat in the following fashion:-

Bob Fitzoffley (enters whistling). – 'The top of the morning to thee, Frank! What! at breakfast already? At chocolate and the *Morning Post*, like a dowager of sixty? Slang! (*he pokes the servant with his cane*) what has come to thy master, thou Prince of Valets! thou pattern of Slaveys! thou swiftest of Mercuries! Has the Honourable Francis Nightrake lost his heart, or his head, or his health?'

Frank (laying down the paper). – 'Bob, Bob, I have lost all three! I have lost my health, Bob, with thee and thy like, over the Burgundy at the club; I have lost my head, Bob, with thinking how I shall pay my debts; and I have lost my heart, Bob, oh, to such a creature!'

Frank. – 'A Venus, of course?'

Slang. – 'With the presence of Juno.'

Bob. – 'And the modesty of Minerva.'

Frank. – 'And the coldness of Diana.'

Bob. – 'Pish! What a sigh is that about a woman! Thou shalt be Endymion, the nightrake of old: and conquer this shy goddess. Hey, Slang?'

Herewith Slang takes the lead of the conversation, and propounds a plot for running away with the heiress; and I could not help remarking how like the comedy was to life – how the gentlemen always say 'thou', and 'prythee', and 'go to', and talk about heathen goddesses to each other; how their servants are always their particular intimates; how when there is serious love-making between a gentleman and lady, a comic attach-ment invariably springs up between the valet and waiting-maid of each; how Lady Grace Gadabout, when she calls upon Rose Ringdove to pay a morning visit, appears in a low satin dress, with jewels in her hair; how Saucebox, her attendant, wears diamond brooches, and rings on all her fingers: while Mrs Tallyho, on the other hand, transacts all the business of life in a riding-habit, and always points her jokes by a cut of the whip.

This playfulness produced a roar all over the house, whenever it was repeated, and always made our little friends clap their hands and shout in chorus.

Like that *bon-vivant* who envied the beggars staring into the cookshop windows, and wished he could be hungry, I envied the boys, and wished I could laugh, very much. In the last act, I remember – for it is now very nearly a week ago – everybody took refuge either in a secret door, or behind a screen or curtain, or under a table, or up a chimney: and the house roared as each person came out from his place of concealment. And the old fellow in top-boots, joining the hands of the young couple (Fitzoffley, of course, pairing off with the widow), gave them his blessing, and thirty thousand pounds.

And ah, ye gods! if I wished before that comedies were like life, how I wished that life was like comedies! Whereon the drop fell; and Augustus, clapping to the opera-glass, jumped up, crying – 'Hurray! now for the Pantomime.'

III

he composer of the Overture of the New Grand Comic Christmas Pantomime, *Harlequin and the Fairy of the Spangled Pocket-handkerchief, or the Prince of the Enchanted Nose*, arrayed in a brand-new Christmas suit, with his wristbands and collar turned elegantly over his cuffs and embroidered satin tie, takes a place at his desk, waves his stick, and away the Pantomime Overture begins.

I pity a man who can't appreciate a Pantomime Overture. Children do not like it: they say, 'Hang it, I wish the Pantomime would begin': but for us it is always a pleasant moment of reflection and enjoyment. It is not difficult music to understand, like that of your Mendelssohns and Beethovens, whose symphonies and sonatas Mrs Spec states must be heard a score of times before you can comprehend them. But of the proper Pantomime-music I am a delighted connoisseur. Perhaps it is because you meet so many old friends in these compositions consorting together in the queerest manner, and occasioning numberless pleasant surprises. Hark! there goes '*Old Dan Tucker*' wandering into the '*Groves of Blarney*'; our friends the '*Scots wha hae wi Wallace bled*' march rapidly down '*Wapping Old Stairs*', from which the

178

'*Figlia del Reggimento*' comes bounding briskly, when she is met, embraced, and carried off by '*Billy Taylor*', that brisk young fellow.

All this while you are thinking with a faint, sickly kind of hope, that perhaps the Pantomime *may* be a good one; something like *Harlequin and the Golden Orange-Tree*, which you recollect in your youth; something like *Fortunio*, that marvellous and delightful piece of buffoonery, which realized the most gorgeous visions of the absurd. You may be happy, perchance: a glimpse of the old days may come back to you. Lives there the man with soul so dead, the being ever so *blasé* and travel-worn, who does not feel some shock and thrill still: just at that moment when the bell (the dear and familiar bell of your youth) begins to tinkle, and the curtain to rise, and the large shoes and ankles, the flesh-coloured leggings, the crumpled knees, the gorgeous robes and masks finally, of the actors ranged on the stage to shout the opening chorus?

All round the house you hear a great gasping a-ha-a from a thousand children's throats. Enjoyment is going to give place to Hope. Desire is about to be realized. O you blind little brats! Clap your hands, and crane over the boxes, and open your eyes with happy wonder! Clap your hands now. In three weeks more the Reverend Doctor Swishtail expects the return of his young friends to Sugarcane House.

* * * * * *

King Beak, Emperor of the Romans, having invited all the neighbouring Princes, Fairies, and Enchanters to the feast at which he celebrated the marriage of his only son, *Prince Aquiline*, unluckily gave the liver-wing of the fowl which he was carving to the Prince's godmother, the *Fairy Bandanna*, while he put the gizzard-pinion on the plate of the *Enchanter Gorgibus*, King of the Maraschino Mountains, and father of the *Princess Rosolia*, to whom the Prince was affianced.

The outraged *Gorgibus* rose from the table in a fury, smashed his plate of chicken over the head of *King Beak's* Chamberlain, and wished that *Prince Aquiline's* nose might grow on the instant as long as the sausage before him.

It did so; the screaming Princess rushed away from her

bridegroom, and her father, breaking off the match with the House of *Beak*, ordered his daughter to be carried in his sedan by the two giant-porters, *Gor* and *Gogstay*, to his castle in the Juniper Forest, by the side of the bitter waters of the Absinthine Lake, whither, after upsetting the marriage-tables, and flooring *King Beak* in a single combat, he himself repaired.

The latter monarch could not bear to see or even to hear his disfigured son.

When the *Prince Aquiline* blew his unfortunate and monstrous nose, the windows of his father's palace broke; the locks of the doors started; the dishes and glasses of the King's banquet jingled and smashed as they do on board a steamboat in a storm; the liquor turned sour; the Chancellor's wig started off his head, and the Prince's royal father, disgusted with his son's appearance, drove him forth from his palace, and banished him the kingdom.

Life was a burden to him on account of that nose. He fled from a world in which he was ashamed to show it, and would have preferred a perfect solitude, but that he was obliged to engage one faithful attendant to give him snuff (his only consolation) and to keep his odious nose in order.

But as he was wandering in a lonely forest, entangling his miserable trunk in the thickets, and causing the birds to fly scared from the branches, and the lions, stags, and foxes to sneak away in terror as they heard the tremendous booming which issued from the fated Prince whenever he had occasion to use his pocket-handkerchief, the Fairy of Bandanna Islands took pity on him, and, descending in her car drawn by doves, gave him a 'kerchief which rendered him invisible whenever he placed it over his monstrous proboscis.

Having occasion to blow his nose (which he was obliged to do pretty frequently, for he had taken cold while lying out among the rocks and morasses in the rainy miserable nights, so that the peasants, when they heard him snoring fitfully, thought that storms were abroad), at the gates of a castle by which he was passing, the door burst open, and the Irish Giant (afterwards Clown, indeed), came out, and wondering looked about, furious to see no one.

The Prince entered into the castle, and whom should he find there but the *Princess Rosolia*, still plunged in despair. Her father snubbed her perpetually. 'I wish he would snub me!'

exclaimed the Prince, pointing to his own monstrous deformity. In spite of his misfortune, she still remembered her Prince. 'Even with his nose,' the faithful Princess cried, 'I love him more than all the world beside!'

At this declaration of unalterable fidelity, the Prince flung away his handkerchief, and knelt in rapture at the Princess's feet. She was a little scared at first by the hideousness of the distorted being before her – but what will not woman's faith

overcome? Hiding her head on his shoulder (and so losing sight of his misfortune), she vowed to love him still (in those broken verses which only Princesses in Pantomimes deliver).

At this instant *King Gorgibus*, the Giants, the King's Household, with clubs and battleaxes, rushed in. Drawing his immense scimitar, and seizing the Prince by his too-prominent feature, he was just on the point of sacrificing him, when – when, I need not say, the *Fairy Bandanna* (Miss Bendigo), in her amaranthine car drawn by Paphian doves, appeared and put a stop to the massacre. *King Gorgibus* became Pantaloon, the two Giants first and second Clowns, and the Prince and Princess (who had been, all the time of the Fairy's speech, and actually while under their father's scimitar, unhooking their dresses) became the most elegant Harlequin and Columbine that I have seen for many a long day. The nose flew up to the ceiling, the music began a jig, and the two Clowns, after saying, 'How are you?' went and knocked down Pantaloon.

IV

n the conclusion of the pantomime, the present memorialist had the honour to conduct the ladies under his charge to the portico of the theatre, where the green fly was in waiting to receive them. The driver was not more inebriated than usual; the young page with the gold-knobbed hat was there to protect his mistresses; and though the chaperon of the party certainly invited me to return with them to Brompton and there drink tea, the proposal was made in terms so faint, and the refreshment offered was so moderate, that I declined to journey six miles on a cold night in order to partake of such a meal. The waterman of the coach-stand, who had made himself conspicuous by bawling out for Mrs Flather's carriage, was importunate with me to give him sixpence for pushing the ladies into the vehicle. But it was my opinion that Mrs Flather ought to settle that demand; and as, while the fellow was urging it, she only pulled up the glass, bidding Cox's man to drive on, I of course did not interfere. In vulgar and immoral language he indicated, as usual, his discontent. I treated the fellow with playful and, I hope, gentlemanlike satire.

Master Jones, who would not leave the box in the theatre until the people came to shroud it with brown-holland, (by the way, to be the last person in a theatre – to put out the last light – and then to find one's way out of the vast, black, lonely place, must require a very courageous heart) – Master Jones, I say, had previously taken leave of us, putting his arm under that of his father's footman, who had been in the pit, and who conducted him to Russell Square. I heard Augustus proposing to have oysters as they went home, though he had twice in the course of the performance made excursions to the cake-room of the theatre, where he had partaken of oranges, macaroons, apples, and ginger beer.

As the altercation between myself and the linkman was going on, young Grigg (brother of Grigg of the Lifeguards, himself reading for the Bar) came up, and hooking his arm into mine, desired the man to leave off 'chaffing' me; asked him if he would take a bill at three months for the money; told him if he would call at the 'Horns Tavern', Kennington, next Tuesday week, he would find sixpence there, done up for him in a brown paper parcel; and quite routed my opponent. 'I know *you*, Mr Grigg,' said he; 'you're a gentleman, *you* are': and so retired, leaving the victory with me.

Young Mr Grigg is one of those young bucks about town, who goes every night of his life to two theatres, to the Casino, to Weippert's balls, to the Café de l'Haymarket, to Bob Slogger's, the boxing-house, to the Harmonic Meetings at the 'Kidney Cellars', and other places of fashionable resort. He knows everybody at these haunts of pleasure; takes boxes for the actors' benefits; has the word from headquarters about the *venue* of the fight between Putney Sambo and the Tutbury Pet; gets up little dinners at their public houses; shoots pigeons, fights cocks, plays fives, has a boat on the river, and a room at Rummer's in Conduit Street, besides his Chambers at the Temple, where his parents, Sir John and Lady Grigg, of Portman Square, and Grigsby Hall, Yorkshire, believe that he is assiduously occupied in studying the Law. 'Tom applies too

much,' her ladyship says. 'His father was obliged to remove
him from Cambridge on account of a brain fever brought on
by hard reading, and in consequence of the jealousy of some of
the collegians; otherwise, I am told, he must have been Senior
Wrangler, and seated first of the Tripod.'

'I'm going to begin the evening,' said this ingenuous young
fellow; 'I've only been at the Lowther Arcade, Weippert's
hop, and the billard rooms. I just toddled in for half an hour to
see Brooke in *Othello*, and looked in for a few minutes behind
the scenes at the Adelphi. What shall be the next resort of
pleasure, Spec, my elderly juvenile? Shall it be the "Sherry-
Cobbler Stall", or the "Cave of Harmony?" There's some
prime glee-singing there.'

'What! is the old "Cave of Harmony" still extant?' I asked.
'I have not been there these twenty years.' And memory
carried me back to the days when Lightsides of Corpus,
myself, and little Paks, the Johnian, came up to town in a
chaise-and-four, at the long vacation at the end of our
freshman's year, ordered turtle and venison for dinner at the
'Bedford', blubbered over *Black-eyed Susan* at the play, and
then finished the evening at that very Harmonic Cave, where
the famous English Improvisatore sang with such prodigious
talent that we asked him down to stay with us in the country.
Spurgin, and Hawker, the fellow-commoner of our College,
I remember me, were at the Cave too, and Bardolph, of
Brasenose. Lord, lord! what a battle and struggle and wear
and tear of life there has been since then! Hawker levanted,
and Spurgin is dead these ten years; little Oaks is a whiskered
Captain of Heavy Dragoons, who cut down no end of Sikhs
at Sobraon; Lightsides, a Tractarian parson, who turns his
head and walks another way when we meet; and your
humble servant – well, never mind. But in my spirit I saw
them – all those blooming and jovial young boys – and
Lightsides, with a cigar in his face, and a bang-up white coat,
covered with mother-of-pearl cheese-plates, bellowing out
for 'First and Second Turn-out', as our yellow postchaise
came rattling up to the inn door at Ware.

'And so the "Cave of Harmony" is open,' I said, looking at
little Grigg with a sad and tender interest, and feeling that I
was about a hundred years old.

'*I believe you, my baw-aw-oy!*' said he, adopting the tone of an exceedingly refined and popular actor, whose choral and comic powers render him a general favourite.

'Does Bivins keep it?' I asked, in a voice of profound melancholy.

'Hoh! What a flat you are! You might as well ask if Mrs Siddons acted *Lady Macbeth* tonight, and if Queen Anne's dead or not. I tell you what, Spec, my boy – you're getting a regular old flat – fogy, sir, a positive old fogy. How the deuce do *you* pretend to be a man about town, and not know that Bivins has left the Cavern? Law bless you! Come in and see: I know the landlord – I'll introduce you to him.'

This was an offer which no man could resist; and so Grigg and I went through the Piazza, and down the steps of that well-remembered place of conviviality. Grigg knew everybody; wagged his head in at the bar, and called for two glasses of his particular mixture; nodded to the singers; winked at one friend – put his little stick against his nose as a token of recognition to another; and calling the waiter by his Christian name, poked him playfully with the end of his cane, and asked him whether he, Grigg, should have a lobster kidney, or a mashed oyster and scalloped 'taters, or a poached rabbit, for supper.

The room was full of young rakish-looking lads, with a dubious sprinkling of us middle-aged youth, and stalwart red-faced fellows from the country, with whisky-noggins before them, and bent upon seeing life. A grand piano had been introduced into the apartment, which did not exist in the old days: otherwise, all was as of yore – smoke rising from scores of human chimneys, waiters bustling about with cigars and liquors in the intervals of the melody – and the President of the meeting (Bivins no more) encouraging gents to give their orders.

Just as the music was about to begin, I looked opposite me, and there, by heavens! sat Bardolph, of Brasenose, only a little more purple and a few shades more dingy than he used to look twenty years ago.

ook at that old Greek in the cloak and fur collar opposite,' said my friend, Mr Grigg. 'That chap is here every night. They call him Lord Farintosh. He has five glasses of whisky-and-water every night – seventeen hundred and twenty-five goes of alcohol in a year; we totted it up one night at the bar. James the waiter is now taking number three to him. He don't count the wine he has had at dinner.' Indeed, James the waiter, knowing the gentleman's peculiarities, as soon as he saw Mr Bardolph's glass nearly empty, brought him another noggin and a jug of boiling water without a word.

Memory carried me instantaneously back to the days of my youth. I had the honour of being at school with Bardolph before he went to Brasenose; the under boys used to look up at him from afar off, as at a godlike being. He was one of the head boys of the school; a prodigious dandy in pigeon-hole trousers, ornamented with what they called 'tucks' in front. He wore a ring – leaving the little finger on which he wore the jewel out of his pocket, in which he carried the rest of his hand. He had whiskers even then: and to this day I cannot understand why he is not seven feet high. When he shouted out, 'Under boy!' we small ones trembled and came to him. I recollect he called me once from a hundred yards off, and I came up in a tremor. He pointed to the ground.

'Pick up my honey-stick,' he said, pointing towards it with the hand with the ring on! He had dropped the stick. He was too great, wise, and good, to stoop to pick it up himself.

He got the silver medal for Latin Sapphics, in the year Pogram was gold medalist. When he went up to Oxford, the Head Master, the Rev J. Flibber, complimented him in a valedictory speech, made him a present of books, and prophesied that he would do great things at the University. He had got a scholarship, and won a prize poem, which the Doctor read out to the sixth form with great emotion. It was on 'The Recollections of Childhood', and the last lines were, –

'Qualia prospiciens catulus ferit aethera risu,
Ipsaque trans lunae cornua vacca salit.'

I thought of these things rapidly, gazing on the individual before me. The brilliant young fellow of 1815 (by the by it was the Waterloo year, by which some people may remember it better; but at school we spoke of years as 'Pogram's year', 'Tokely's year', &c.) – there, I say, sat before me the dashing young buck of 1815, a fat, muzzy, red-faced old man, in a battered hat, absorbing whisky-and-water, and half listening to the singing.

A wild, long-haired, professional gentleman, with a fluty voice and with his shirt collar turned down, began to sing as follows:–

'WHEN THE GLOOM IS ON THE GLEN

'When the moonlight's on the mountain
    And the gloom is on the glen,
At the cross beside the fountain
    There is one will meet thee then.
At the cross beside the fountain;
    Yes, the cross beside the fountain,
There is one will meet thee then!

[*Down goes half of* Mr Bardolph's *No. 3 Whisky during this refrain.*]

'I have braved, since first we met, love,
    Many a danger in my course;
But I never can forget, love,
    That dear fountain, that old cross,
Where, her mantle shrouded o'er her
    For the winds were chilly then –
First I met my Leonora,
    When the gloom was on the glen,
    Yes, I met my &c.

[*Another gulp and almost total disappearance of Whisky Go, No. 3.*]

'Many a clime I've ranged since then, love,
    Many a land I've wandered o'er;
But a valley like that glen, love,

Half so dear I never sor!
Ne'er saw maiden fairer, coyer,
   Than wert thou, my true love, when
In the gloaming first I saw yer,
   In the gloaming of the glen!'

Bardolph, who had not shown the least symptom of emotion as the gentleman with the fluty voice performed this delectable composition, began to whack, whack, whack on the mahogany with his pewter measure at the conclusion of the song, wishing, perhaps, to show that the noggin was empty; in which manner, James, the waiter, interpreted the signal, for he brought Mr Bardolph another supply of liquor.

The song, words, and music, composed and dedicated to Charles Bivins, Esquire, by Frederic Snape, and ornamented with a picture of a young lady, with large eyes and short petticoats, leaning at a stone cross by a fountain, and now handed about the room by a waiter, and any gentleman was at liberty to purchase it for half a crown. The man did not offer the song to Bardolph; he was too old a hand.

After a pause, the president of the musical gents cried out for silence again, and then stated to the company that Mr Hoff would sing '*The Red Flag*', which announcement was received by the Society with immense applause, and Mr Hoff, a gentleman whom I remember to have seen exceedingly unwell on board a Gravesend steamer, began the following terrific ballad:–

'THE RED FLAG

'Where the quivering lighting flings
   His arrows from out of the clouds,
And the howling tempest sings,
   And whistles among the shrouds,
'Tis pleasant, 'tis pleasant to ride
   Along the foaming brine –
Wilt be the Rover's bride?
   Wilt follow him, lady mine?
     Hurrah!
For the bonny, bonny brine.

'Amidst the storm and rack,
   You shall see our galley pass
As a serpent, lithe and black,
   Glides through the waving grass.
As the vulture swift and dark,
   Down on the ring-dove flies,
You shall see the Rover's bark
   Swoop down upon his prize.
        Hurrah!
For the bonny, bonny prize.

'Over her sides we dash,
   We gallop across her deck –
Ha! there's a ghastly gash
   On the merchant-captain's neck –
Well shot, well shot, old Ned!
   Well struck, well struck, black James!
Our arms are red, and our foes are dead,
   And we leave a ship in flames!
        Hurrah!
For the bonny, bonny flames!'

Frantic shouts of applause and encore hailed the atrocious
sentiments conveyed by Mr Hoff in this ballad, from everybody except Bardolph, who sat muzzy and unmoved, and
only winked to the waiter to bring him some more whisky.

A NIGHT'S PLEASURE

VI

hen the piratical ballad of Mr Hoff was concluded, a simple and quiet-looking young gentleman performed a comic song, in a way which, I must confess, inspired me with the utmost melancholy. Seated at the table with the other professional gents, this young gentleman was in no way to be distinguished from any other young man of fashion: he has a thin, handsome, and rather sad countenance; and appears to be a perfectly sober and meritorious young man. But suddenly (and I daresay every night of his life) he pulls a little flexible, grey countryman's hat out of his pocket, and the moment he has put it on, his face assumes an expression of unutterable vacuity and folly, his eyes goggle round savage, and his mouth stretches almost to his ears, and he begins to sing a rustic song.

The battle song and the sentimental ballad already published are, I trust, sufficiently foolish, and fair specimens of the class of poetry to which they belong; but the folly of the comic country song was so great and matchless, that I am not going to compete for a moment with the author, or to venture to attempt anything like his style of composition. It was something about a man going-a-courting Molly, and 'feayther', and 'kyows', and 'peegs', and other rustic produce. The idiotic verse was interspersed with spoken passages, of corresponding imbecility. For the time during which Mr Grinsby performed this piece, he consented to abnegate altogether his claim to be considered as a reasonable being; utterly to debase himself, in order to make the company laugh; and to forget the rank, dignity, and privileges of a man.

His song made me so profoundly wretched that little Grigg, remarking my depression, declared I was as slow as a parliamentary train. I was glad they didn't have the song over again. When it was done, Mr Grinsby put his little grey hat in his pocket, the maniacal grin subsided from his features, and he sat down with his naturally sad and rather handsome young countenance.

WITHOUT HIS HAT.   IN HIS COMIC HAT.

O Grinsby, thinks I, what a number of people and things in this world do you represent! Though we weary listening to you, we may moralise over you; though you sing a foolish, witless song, you poor young melancholy jester, there is some good in it that may be had for the seeking. Perhaps that lad has a family at home dependent on his grinning: I may entertain a reasonable hope that he has despair in his heart; a complete notion of the folly of the business in which he is engaged; a contempt for the fools laughing and guffawing round about at his miserable jokes; and a perfect weariness of mind at their original dullness and continued reception. What a sinking of spirit must come over that young man, quiet in his chamber or family, orderly and sensible like other mortals, when the thought of tomfool hour comes across him, and that at a certain time that night, whatever may be his health, or distaste, or mood of mind or body, there he must be, at a table at the 'Cave of Harmony', uttering inane ballads, with an idiotic grin on his face and hat on his head.

To suppose that Grinsby has any personal pleasure in that song, would be to have too low an opinion of human nature: to imagine that the applauses of the multitude of the frequenters of the Cave tickled his vanity, or are bestowed upon him deservedly – would be, I say, to think too hardly of him. Look at him. He sits there quite a quiet, orderly young fellow. Mark with what an abstracted, sad air he joins in the chorus of Mr Snape's second song, 'The Minaret's bells o'er the Bosphorus toll', and having applauded his comrade at the end of the song (as I have remarked these poor gentlemen always do), moodily resumes the stump of his cigar.

'I wonder, my dear Grigg, how many men there are in the city who follow a similar profession to Grinsby's? What a number of poor rogues, wits in their circle, or bilious, or in debt, or henpecked, or otherwise miserable in their private circumstances, come grinning out to dinner of a night, and laugh and crack, and let off their good stories like yonder professional funny fellow? Why, I once went into the room of that famous dinner-party conversationalist and wit, Horsely Collard; and whilst he was in his dressing-room arranging his wig, just looked over the books on the table before his sofa. There were "Burton's Anatomy" for the quotations, three of which he let off that night; "Spence's Literary Anecdotes", of which he fortuitously introduced a couple in the course of the evening; "Baker's Chronicle"; the last new Novel, and a book of Metaphysics, every one of which I heard him quote, besides four stories out of his commonplace book, at which I took a peep under the pillow. He was like Grinsby.' Who isn't like Grinsby in life? thought I to myself, examining that young fellow.

'When Bawler goes down to the House of Commons from a meeting with his creditors, and having been a bankrupt a month before, becomes a patriot all of a sudden, and pours you out an intensely interesting speech upon the West Indies, or the Window Tax, he is not better than the poor gin-and-water practitioner yonder, and performs in his Cave, as Grinsby in his under the Piazza.

'When Sergeant Bluebag fires into a witness, or performs a jocular or a pathetic speech to a jury, in what is he better than Grinsby, except in so far as the amount of gain goes? – than poor Grinsby, rapping at the table and cutting professional jokes, at half-a-pint-of-whisky fee?

'When Tightrope, the celebrated literary genius, sits down to write and laugh – with the children very likely ill at home – with a strong personal desire to write a tragedy or a sermon, with his wife scolding him, his head racking with pain, his mother-in-law making a noise at his ears, and telling him that he is a heartless and abandoned ruffian, his tailor in the passage, vowing that he will not quit that place until his little bill is settled – when, I say, Tightrope writes off, under the most miserable private circumsances, a brilliant funny article, in how much is he morally superior to my friend Grinsby? When Lord Colchicum stands bowing and smiling before his sovereign, with gout in his toes, and grief in his heart; when parsons in the pulpit – when editors at their desks – forget their natural griefs, pleasures, opinions, to go through the business of life, the masquerade of existence, in what are they better than Grinsby yonder, who has similarly to perform his buffooning?'

As I was continuing in this moral and interrogatory mood – no doubt boring poor little Grigg, who came to the Cave for pleasure, and not for philosophical discourse – Mr Bardolph opposite caught a sight of the present writer through the fumes of the cigars, and came across to our table, holding his fourth glass of toddy in his hand. He held out the other to me: it was hot, and gouty, and not particularly clean.

'Deuced queer place this, hey?' said he, pretending to survey it with the air of a stranger. 'I come here every now and then, on my way home to Lincoln's Inn – from – from parties at the other end of the town. It is frequented by a parcel of queer people – low shop-boys and attorneys' clerks; but hang it, sir, they know a gentleman when they see one, and not one of those fellows would dare to speak to me – no, not one of 'em, by Jove – if I didn't address him first, by Jove! I don't suppose there's a man in this room could construe a page in the commonest Greek book. You heard that donkey singing about "Leonorar" and "before her"? How Flibber would have given it to us for such rhymes, hey? A parcel of ignoramuses! but, hang it, sir, they *do* know a gentleman!' And here he winked at me with a vinous bloodshot eye, as much as to intimate that he was infinitely superior to every person in the room.

Now this Bardolph, having had the ill-luck to get a fellowship, and subsequently a small private fortune, had done nothing since the year 1820 but get drunk and read Greek. He despises every man that does not know that language (so that you and I, my dear sir, come in for a fair share of his contempt). He can still put a slang song into Greek Iambics, or turn a police report into the language of Tacitus or Herodotus; but it is difficult to see what accomplishment beyond this the boozy old mortal possesses. He spends nearly a third part of his life and income at his dinner, or on his whisky at a tavern; more than another third portion is spent in bed. It is past noon before he gets up to breakfast, and to spell over *The Times*, which business of the day being completed, it is time for him to dress and take his walk to the Club to dinner. He scorns a man who puts his *h*'s in the wrong place, and spits at a human being who has not had a University education. And yet I am sure that bustling waiter pushing about with a bumper of cigars; that tallow-faced young comic singer; yonder harmless and happy Snobs, enjoying the conviviality of the evening (and all the songs are quite modest now, not like the ribald old ditties which they used to sing in former days), are more useful, more honouable, and more worthy men, than that whiskyfied old scholar who looks down upon them and their like.

He said he would have a sixth glass if we would stop: but we didn't; and he took his sixth glass without us. My melancholy young friend had begun another comic song, and I could bear it no more. The market carts were rattling into Covent Garden; and the illuminated clock marked all sorts of small hours as we concluded this night's pleasure.

GOING TO SEE A MAN HANGED[*]

July, 1840

 —, who had voted with Mr Ewart for the abolition of the punishment of death, was anxious to see the effect on the public mind of an execution, and asked me to accompany him to see Courvoisier killed. We had not the advantage of a sheriff's order, like the 'six hundred noblemen and gentlemen' who were admitted within the walls of the prison; but determined to mingle with the crowd at the foot of the scaffold, and take up our positions at a very early hour.

As I was to rise at three in the morning, I went to bed at ten, thinking that five hours' sleep would be amply sufficient to brace me against the fatigues of the coming day. But, as might have been expected, the event of the morrow was perpetually before my eyes through the night, and kept them wide open. I heard all the clocks in the neighbourhood chime the hours in succession; a dog from some court hard by kept up a pitiful howling; at one o'clock, a cock set up a feeble, melancholy crowing; shortly after two the daylight came peeping grey through the window shutters; and by the time that X— arrived, in fulfilment of his promise, I had been asleep about half an hour. He, more wise, had not gone to rest at all, but

[*] Originally published in *Fraser's Magazine*.

had remained up all night at the Club, along with Dash and two or three more. Dash is one of the most eminent wits in London, and had kept the company merry all night with appropriate jokes about the coming event. It is curious that a murder is a great inspirer of jokes. We all like to laugh and have our fling about it; there is a certain grim pleasure in the circumstance – a perpetual jingling antithesis between life and death, that is sure of its effect.

In mansion or garret, on down or straw, surrounded by weeping friends and solemn oily doctors, or tossing unheeded upon scanty hospital beds, there were many people in this great city to whom that Sunday night was to be the last of any that they should pass on earth here. In the course of half a dozen dark, wakeful hours, one had leisure to think of these (and a little, too, of that certain supreme night, that shall come at one time or other, when he who writes shall be stretched upon the last bed, prostrate in the last struggle, taking the last look of dear faces that have cheered us here, and lingering – one moment more – ere we part for the tremendous journey); but, chiefly, I could not help thinking, as each clock sounded, what is *he* doing now? has *he* heard it in his little room in Newgate yonder? Eleven o'clock. He has been writing until now. The gaoler says he is a pleasant man enough to be with; but he can hold out no longer, and is very weary. 'Wake me at four', says he, 'for I have still much to put down.' From eleven to twelve the gaoler hears how he is grinding his teeth in his sleep. At twelve he is up in his bed, and asks, 'Is it the time?' He has plenty more time yet for sleep; and he sleeps, and the bell goes on tolling. Seven hours more – five hours more. Many a carriage is clattering through the streets, bringing ladies away from evening parties; many bachelors are reeling home after a jolly night; Covent Garden is alive and the light coming through the cell window turns the gaoler's candle pale. Four hours more! 'Courvoisier', says the gaoler, shaking him, 'it's four o'clock now, and I've woke you as you told me; but there's no call for you *to get up yet.*' The poor wretch leaves his bed, however, and makes his last toilet; and then falls to writing, to tell the world how he did the crime for which he has suffered. This time he will tell the truth, and the whole truth. They bring him his breakfast 'from the coffee shop opposite – tea, coffee, and thin bread and butter.' He will take nothing, however, but goes on writing. He has to write to his mother – the pious mother far away in his own country – who reared him and loved him; and even now has sent him her forgiveness and her blessing. He finishes his memorials and letters, and makes his will, disposing of his little miserable property of books and tracts that pious people have furnished him with. '*Ce 6 Juillet, 1840. François Benjamin Courvoisier vous donne ceci, mon ami, pour souvenir.*' He has a token for his dear friend the gaoler; another for his dear friend the under-sheriff. As the day of the convict's death draws nigh, it is painful to see how he fastens upon everybody who approaches him, how pitifully he clings to them and loves them.

While these things are going on within the prison (with which we are made accurately acquainted by the copious chronicles of such events which are published subsequently), X—'s carriage has driven up to the door of my lodgings, and we have partaken of an elegant *déjeuner* that has been prepared for the occasion. A cup of coffee at half past three in the morning is uncommonly pleasant; and X— enlivens us with the repetition of the jokes that Dash has just been making. Admirable, certainly – they must have had a merry night of it, that's clear; and we stoutly debate whether, when one has to get up so early in the morning, it is best to have an hour or two of sleep, or wait and go to bed afterwards at the end of the day's work. That fowl is extraordinarily tough – the wing, even, is as hard as a board; a slight disappointment, for there is nothing else for breakfast. 'Will any gentleman have some sherry and soda water before he sets out? It clears the brains famously.' Thus primed, the party sets out. The coachman has dropped a sleep on the box, and wakes up wildly as the hall door opens. It is just four o'clock. About this very time they are waking up poor – pshaw! who is for a cigar? X— does not smoke himelf; but vows and protests, in the kindest way in the world, that he does not care in the least for the new drab-silk linings in his carriage. Z—, who smokes, mounts, however, the box. 'Drive to Snow Hill,' says the owner of the chariot. The policemen, who are the only people in the street, and are standing by, look knowing – they know what it means well enough.

How cool and clean the streets look, as the carriage startles the echoes that have been asleep in the corners all night. Somebody has been sweeping the pavements clean in the night-time surely; they would not soil a lady's white satin shoes, they are so dry and neat. There is not a cloud or a breath in the air, except Z—'s cigar, which whiffs off, and soars straight upwards in volumes of white, pure smoke. The trees in the squares look bright and green – as bright as leaves in the country in June. We who keep late hours don't know the beauty of London air and verdure; in the early morning they are delightful – the most fresh and lively companions possible. But they cannot bear the crowd and the bustle of midday. You don't know them then – they are no longer the same things. We have come to Gray's Inn; there is actually dew upon the grass in the gardens; and the windows of the stout old red houses are all in a flame.

As we enter Holborn the town grows more animated; and there are already twice as many people in the streets as you see at midday in a German *Residenz* or an English provincial town. The ginshop keepers have many of them taken their shutters down, and many persons are issuing from them pipe in hand. Down they go along the broad bright street, their blue shadows marching *after* them; for they are all bound the same way, and are bent like us upon seeing the hanging.

It is twenty minutes past four as we pass St Sepulchre's: by this time many hundred people are in the street, and many more are coming up Snow Hill. Before us lies Newgate Prison; but something a great deal more awful to look at, which seizes the eye at once, and makes the heart beat, is

There it stands black and ready, jutting out from a little door in the prison. As you see it, you feel a kind of dumb

electric shock, which causes one to start a little, and give a sort of gasp for breath. The shock is over in a second; and presently you examine the object before you with a certain feeling of complacent curiosity. At least, such was the effect that the gallows produced upon the writer, who is trying to set down all his feelings as they occurred, and not to exaggerate them at all.

After the gallows-shock had subsided, we went down into the crowd, which was very numerous, but not dense as yet. It was evident that the day's *business* had not begun. People sauntered up, and formed groups, and talked; the new comers asking those who seemed *habitués* of the place about former executions; and did the victim hang with his face towards the clock or towards Ludgate Hill? and had he the rope round his neck when he came on the scaffold, or was it put on by Jack Ketch afterwards? and had Lord W— taken a window, and which was he? I may mention the noble Marquis's name, as he was not at the exhibition. A psuedo W— was pointed out in an opposite window, towards whom all the people in our neighbourhood looked eagerly, and with great respect too. The mob seemed to have no sort of ill-will against him, but sympathy and admiration. The noble lord's personal courage and strength have won the plebs over to him. Perhaps his exploits against policemen have occasioned some of this popularity; for the mob hate them, as children the school-master.

Throughout the whole four hours, however, the mob was extraordinarily gentle and good-humoured. At first we had leisure to talk to the people about us; and I recommend X—'s brother senators of both sides of the House to see more of this same people and to appreciate them better. Honourable Members are battling and struggling in the House; shouting, yelling, crowing, hear-hearing, pooh-poohing, making speeches of three columns, and gaining 'great Conservative triumphs', or 'signal successes of the Reform cause', as the case may be. Three hundred and ten gentlemen of good fortune, and able for the most part to quote Horace, declare solemnly that unless Sir Robert comes in, the nation is ruined. Three hundred and fifteen on the other side swear by their great gods that the safety of the empire depends upon Lord

John; and to this end they quote Horace too. I declare that I have never been in a great London crowd without thinking of what they call the two 'great' parties in England with wonder. For which of the two great leaders do these people care, I pray you? When Lord Stanley withdrew his Irish bill the other night, were they in transports of joy, like worthy persons who read the *Globe* and the *Chronicle*? or when he beat the Ministers, were they wild with delight, like honest gentlemen who read the *Post* and the *Times*? Ask yonder ragged fellow, who has evidently frequented debating clubs, and speaks with good sense and shrewd good nature. He cares no more for Lord John than he does for Sir Robert; and, with due respect be it said, would mind very little if both of them were ushered out by Mr Ketch, and took their places under yonder black beam. What are the two great parties to him, and those like him? Sheer wind, hollow humbug, absurd claptraps; a silly mummery of dividing and debating, which does not in the least, however it may turn, affect his condition. It has been so ever since the happy days when Whigs and Tories began; and a pretty pastime no doubt it is for both. August parties, great balances of British freedom: are not the two sides quite as active, and eager, and loud, as at their very birth, and ready to fight for place as stoutly as ever they fought before? But lo! in the meantime, whilst you are jangling and brawling over the accounts, *Populus*, whose estate you have administered while he was an infant, and could not take care of himself – Populus has been growing and growing, till he is every bit as wise as his guardians. Talk to our ragged friend. He is not so polished, perhaps, as a member of the 'Oxford and Cambridge Club'; he has not been to Eton; and never read Horace in his life: but he can think just as soundly as the best of you; he can speak quite as strongly in his own rough way; he has been reading all sorts of books of late years, and gathered together no little information. He is as good a man as the common run of us; and there are ten million more men in the country as good as he – ten million, for whom we, in our infinite superiority, are acting as guardians, and to whom, in our bounty, we give – exactly nothing. Put yourself in their position, worthy sir. You and a hundred others find yourselves in some lone place, where you set up a government. You take a chief, as is natural;

he is the cheapest order-keeper in the world. You establish half a dozen worthies, whose families you say shall have the privilege to legislate for you for ever; half a dozen more, who shall be appointed by a choice of thirty of the rest: and the other sixty, who shall have no choice, vote, place, or privilege, at all. Honourable sir, suppose that you are one of the last sixty: how will you feel, you who have intelligence, passions, honest pride, as well as your neighbour; how will you feel towards your equals, in whose hands lie all the power and all the property of the community? Would you love and honour them, tamely acquiesce in their superiority, see their privileges, and go yourself disregarded without a pang? you are not a man if you would. I am not talking of right or wrong, or debating questions of government. But ask my friend there, with the ragged elbows and no shirt, what he thinks? You have your party, Conservative or Whig, as it may be. You believe that an aristocracy is an institution necessary, beautiful, and virtuous. You are a gentleman, in other words, and stick by your party.

And our friend with the elbows (the crowd is thickening hugely all this time) sticks by *his*. Talk to him of Whig or Tory, he grins at them: of virtual representation, pish! He is a *democrat*, and will stand by his friends, as you by yours; and they are twenty millions, his friends, of whom a vast minority now, a majority a few years hence, will be as good as you. In the meantime we shall continue electing, and debating, and dividing, and having every day new triumphs for the glorious cause of Conservatism, or the glorious cause of Reform, until—

*   *   *   *   *   *

What is the meaning of this unconscionable republican tirade – *àpropos* of a hanging? Such feelings, I think, must come across any man in a vast multitude like this. What good sense and intelligence have most of the people by whom you are surrounded; how much sound humour does one hear bandied about from one to another! A great number of coarse phrases are used, that would make ladies in drawing-rooms blush; but the morals of the men are good and hearty. A ragamuffin in the crowd (a powdery baker in a white sheep's-wool cap) uses some indecent expression to a woman near: there is an instant cry of shame, which silences the man, and a dozen people are ready to give the woman protection. The crowd has grown very dense by this time, it is about six o'clock, and there is great heaving, and pushing, and swaying to and fro; but round the women the men have formed a circle, and keep them as much as possible out of the rush and trample. In one of the houses near us, a gallery has been formed on the roof. Seats were here let, and a number of persons of various degrees were occupying them. Several tipsy, dissolute-looking young men, of the Dick Swiveller cast, were in this gallery. One was lolling over the sunshiny tiles, with a fierce sodden face, out of which came a pipe, and which was shaded by long matted hair, and a hat cocked very much on one side. This gentleman was one of a party which had evidently not been to bed on Sunday night, but had passed it in some of those delectable nighthouses in the neighbourhood of Covent Garden. The debauch was not over yet, and the women of the party were giggling, drinking, and romping, as in the wont of these delicate creatures; sprawling here and there, and falling upon the knees of one or other of the males. Their scarves were off their shoulders, and you saw the sun shining down upon the bare white flesh, and the shoulder-points glittering like burning glasses. The people about us were very indignant at some of the proceedings of this debauched crew, and at last raised up such a yell as frightened them into shame, and they were more orderly for the remainder of the day. The windows of the shops opposite began to fill apace, and our before-mentioned friend with ragged elbows pointed out a celebrated fashionable character who occupied one of them; and, to our surprise, knew as much about him as the *Court Journal* or the *Morning Post*. Presently he entertained us with a long and pretty accurate account of the history of Lady —, and indulged in a judicious criticism upon her last work. I have met with many a country gentleman who had not read half as many books as this honest fellow, this shrewd *prolétaire* in a black shirt. The people about him took up and carried on the conversation very knowingly, and were very little behind him in point of information. It was just as good a company as one meets on common occasions. I was in a genteel crowd in one of the galleries at the Queen's coronation; indeed, in point of intelligence, the democrats were quite equal to the aristocrats. How many more such groups were there in this immense multitude of nearly forty thousand, as some say? How many more such throughout the country? I never yet, as I said before, have been in an English mob, without the same feeling for the persons who composed it, and without wonder at the vigorous, orderly good sense and intelligence of the people.

The character of the crowd was as yet, however, quite festive. Jokes bandying about here and there, and jolly laughs breaking out. Some men were endeavouring to climb up a leaden pipe on one of the houses. The landlord came out, and endeavoured with might and main to pull them down. Many thousand eyes turned upon this contest immediately. All sorts of voices issued from the crowd, and uttered choice expressions of slang. When one of the men was pulled down by the leg, the waves of this black mob-ocean laughed innumerably; when one fellow slipped away, scrambled up the pipe, and made good his lodgment on the shelf, we were all made happy, and encouraged him by loud shouts of admiration. What is there so particularly delightful in the spectacle of a man clambering up a gas-pipe? Why were we kept for a quarter of an hour in deep interest gazing upon this remarkable scene? Indeed it is hard to say: a man does not know what a fool he is until he tries; or, at least, what mean follies will amuse him. The other day I went to Astley's, and saw a clown come in with a foolscap and pinafore, and six small boys who represented his schoolfellows. To them enters schoolmaster; horses clown, and flogs him hugely on the back part of his pinafore. I never read anything in Swift, Boz, Rabelais, Fielding, Paul de Kock, which delighted me so much as this sight, and caused me to laugh so profoundly. And why? What is there so ridiculous in the sight of one miserably rouged man beating another on the breech? Tell us where the fun lies in this and the before-mentioned episode of the gas-pipe? Vast, indeed, are the capacities and ingenuities of the human soul that can find, in incidents so wonderfully small, means of contemplation and amusement.

Really the time passed away with extraordinary quickness. A thousand things of the sort related here came to amuse us. First the workmen knocking and hammering at the scaffold, mysterious clattering of blows was heard within it, and a ladder painted black was carried round, and into the interior of the edifice by a small side-door. We all looked at this little ladder and at each other – things began to be very interesting. Soon came a squad of policemen; stalwart, rosy-looking men, saying much for City feeding; well-dressed, well-limbed, and of admirable good humour. They paced about the open space between the prison and the barriers which kept in the crowd from the scaffold. The front line, as far as I could see, was chiefly occupied by blackguards and boys – professional persons, no doubt, who saluted the policemen on their appearance with a volley of jokes and ribaldry. As far as I could judge from faces, there were more blackguards of sixteen and seventeen than of any maturer age; stunted, sallow, ill-grown lads, in rugged fustian, scowling about. There were a considerable number of girls, too, of the same age; one that Cruikshank and Boz might have taken as a study for Nancy. The girl was a young thief's mistress evidently; if attacked, ready to reply without a particle of modesty; could give as good ribaldry as she got; made no secret (and there were several inquiries) as to her profession and means of livelihood. But with all this, there was something good about the girl; a sort of devil-may-care candour and simplicity that one could not fail to see. Her answers to some of the coarse questions put to her, were very ready and good-humoured. She had a friend with her of the same age and class, of whom she seemed to be very fond, and who looked up to her for protection. Both of these women had beautiful eyes. Devil-may-care's were extraordinarily bright and blue, an admirably fair complexion, and a large red mouth full of white teeth. *Au reste*, ugly, stunted, thick-limbed, and by no means a beauty. Her friend could not be more than fifteen. They were not in rags, but had greasy cotton shawls, and old, faded, rag-shop bonnets. I was curious to look at them, having, in late fashionable novels, read many accounts of such personages. Bah! what figments these novelists tell us! Boz, who knows life well, knows that his Miss Nancy is the most unreal fantastical personage possible; no more like a thief's mistress than one of Gesner's shepherdesses resembles a real country wench. He dare not tell the truth concerning such young ladies. They have, no doubt, virtues like other human creatures; nay, their position engenders virtues that are not called into exercise among other women. But on these an honest painter of human nature has no right to dwell; not being able to paint the whole portrait, he has no right to present one or two favourable points as characterizing the whole; and therefore, in fact, had better leave the picture alone altogether. The new French literature is essentially false and worthless from this very error – the writers giving us favourable pictures of monsters, and (to say nothing of decency or morality) pictures quite untrue to nature.

But yonder, glittering through the crowd in Newgate Street – see, the Sheriffs' carriages are slowly making their way. We have been here three hours! Is it possible that they can have passed so soon? Close to the barriers where we are, the mob has become so dense that it is with difficulty a man can keep his feet. Each man, however, is very careful in protecting the women, and all are full of jokes and good humour. The windows of the shops opposite are now pretty nearly filled by the persons who hired them. Many young dandies are there with moustaches and cigars; some quiet, fat, family parties, of simple, honest tradesmen and their wives, as we fancy, who are looking on with the greatest imaginable calmness, and sipping their tea. Yonder is the sham Lord W—, who is flinging various articles among the crowd; one of his companions, a tall, burly man, with large moustaches, has provided himself with a squirt, and is aspersing the mob with brandy-and-water. Honest gentleman! high-bred aristocrat! genuine lover of humour and wit! I would walk some miles to see thee on the treadmill, thee and thy Mohawk crew!

We tried to get up a hiss against these ruffians, but only had a trifling success; the crowd did not seem to think their offence very heinous; and our friend, the philosopher in the ragged elbows, who had remained near us all the time, was not inspired with any such savage disgust at the proceedings of certain notorious young gentlemen, as I must confess fills my own particular bosom. He only said, 'So-and-so is a lord, and they'll let him off', and then discoursed about Lord Ferrers being hanged. The philosopher knew the history pretty well, and so did most of the little knot of persons about him, and it must be a gratifying thing for young gentlemen to find that their actions are made the subject of this kind of conversation.

Scarcely a word had been said about Courvoisier all this time. We were all, as far as I could judge, in just such a frame of mind as men are in when they are squeezing at the pit-door of a play, or pushing for a review or a Lord Mayor's show. We asked most of the men who were near us, whether they had seen many executions? most of them had, the philosopher especially; whether the sight of them did any good? 'For the matter of that, no; people did not care about them at all; nobody ever thought of it after a bit.' A countryman, who had left his drove in Smithfield, said the same thing; he had seen a man hanged at York, and spoke of the ceremony with perfect good sense, and in a quiet, sagacious way.

JS—, the famous wit, now dead, had, I recollect, a good story upon the subject of executing, and of the terror which the punishment inspires. After Thistlewood and his companions were hanged, their heads were taken off, according to the sentence, and the executioner, as he severed each, held it up to the crowd, in the proper orthodox way, saying, 'Here is the head of a traitor!' At the sight of the first ghastly head the people were struck with terror, and a general expression of disgust and fear broke from them. The second head was looked at also with much interest, but the excitement regarding the third head diminished. When the executioner had come to the last of the heads, he lifted it up, but, by some clumsiness, allowed it to drop. At this the crowd yelled out, '*Ah, Butter-fingers!*' – the excitement had passed entirely away. The punishment had grown to be a joke – Butter-fingers was the word – a pretty commentary, indeed, upon the august nature of public executions, and the awful majesty of the law.

It was past seven now; the quarters rang and passed away; the crowd began to grow very eager and more quiet, and we turned back every now and then and looked at St Sepulchre's clock. Half an hour, twenty-five minutes. What is he doing now? He has his irons off by this time. A quarter: he's in the pressroom now, no doubt. Now at last we had come to think about the man we were going to see hanged. How slowly the clock crept over the last quarter! Those who were able to turn round and see (for the crowd was now extraordinarily dense) chronicled the time, eight minutes, five minutes; at last – ding, dong, dong, dong! – the bell is tolling the chimes of eight.

* * * * * *

Between the writing of this line and the last, the pen has been put down, as the reader may suppose, and the person who is addressing him as gone through a pause of no very pleasant thoughts and recollections. The whole of the sickening, ghastly, wicked scene passes before the eyes again; and, indeed, it is an awful one to see, and very hard and painful to describe.

As the clock began to strike, an immense sway and movement swept over the whole of that vast dense crowd. They were all uncovered directly, and a great murmur arose, more awful, bizarre, and indescribable than any sound I had ever before heard. Women and children began to shriek horribly. I don't know whether it was the bell I heard; but a dreadful quick, feverish kind of jangling noise mingled with the noise of the people, and lasted for about two minutes. The scaffold stood before us, tenantless and black; the black chain was hanging down ready from the beam. Nobody came. 'He has been respited', someone said; another said, 'He has killed himself in prison.'

Just then, from under the black prison door, a pale, quiet head peered out. It was shockingly bright and distinct; it rose up directly, and a man in black appeared on the scaffold, and was silently followed by about four more dark figures. The first was a tall grave man: we all knew who the second man was. '*That's he – that's he!*' you heard the people say, as the devoted man came up.

I have seen a cast of the head since, but, indeed, should never have known it. Courvoisier bore his punishment like a man, and walked very firmly. He was dressed in a new black suit, as it seemed: his shirt was open. His arms were tied in front of him. He opened his hands in a helpless kind of way, and clasped them once or twice together. He turned his head here and there, and looked about him for an instant with a wild, imploring look. His mouth was contracted into a sort of pitiful smile. He went and placed himself at once under the beam, with his face towards St Sepulchre's. The tall, grave man in black twisted him round swiftly in the other direction, and, drawing from his pocket a nightcap, pulled it tight over the patient's head and face. I am not ashamed to say that I could look no more, but shut my eyes as the last dreadful act was going on, which sent this wretched guilty soul into the presence of God.

If a public execution is beneficial – and beneficial it is, no doubt, or else the wise laws would not encourage forty thousand people to witness it – the next useful thing must be a full description of such a ceremony, and all its *entourages*, and to this end the above pages are offered to the reader. How does an individual man feel under it? In what way does he observe it, – how does he view all the phenomena connected with it, – what induces him, in the first instance, to go and see it, – and how is he moved by it afterwards? The writer has discarded the magazine 'We' altogether, and spoken face to face with the reader, recording every one of the impressions felt by him as honestly as he could.

I must confess, then (for 'I' is the shortest word, and the best in this case), that the sight has left on my mind an extraordinarily feeling of terror and shame. It seems to me that I have been abetting an act of frightful wickedness and violence, performed by a set of men against one of their fellows; and I pray God that it may soon be out of the power of any man in England to witness such a hideous and degrading sight. Forty thousand persons (say the Sheriffs), of all ranks and degrees, – mechanics, gentlemen, pickpockets, members of both Houses of Parliament, streetwalkers, newspaper writers, gather together before Newgate at a very early hour; the most part of them give up their natural quiet night's rest, in order to partake of this hideous debauchery, which is more exciting than sleep, or than wine, or the last new ballet, or any other amusement they can have. Pickpocket and Peer each is tickled by the sight alike, and has that hidden lust after blood which influences our race. Government, a Christian government, gives us a feast every now and then: it agrees – that is to say – a majority in the two Houses agrees, that for certain crimes it is necessary that a man should be hanged by the neck. Government commits the criminal's soul to the mercy of God, stating that here on earth he is to look for no mercy; keeps him for a fortnight to prepare, provides him with a clergyman to settle his religious matters (if there be time enough, but Government can't wait); and on a Monday morning, the bell tolling, the clergyman reading out the word of God, 'I am the resurrection and the life,' 'The Lord giveth and the Lord taketh away,' – on a Monday morning, at eight o'clock, this man is placed under a beam, with a rope connecting it and him; a plank disappears from under him, and those who have paid for good places may see the hands of the Government agent, Jack Ketch, coming up from his black hole, and seizing the prisoner's legs, and pulling them, until he is quite dead – strangled.

Many persons, and well-informed newspapers, say that it is mawkish sentiment to talk in this way, morbid humanity, cheap philanthropy, that any man can get up and preach about. There is the *Observer*, for instance, a paper conspicuous for the tremendous sarcasm which distinguishes its articles, and which falls cruelly foul of the *Morning Herald*. 'Courvoisier is dead', says the *Observer*; 'he died as he had lived – a villain; a lie was in his mouth. Peace be to his ashes. We war not with the dead.' What a magnanimous *Observer*! From this, *Observer* turns to the *Herald*, and says, '*Fiat justitia ruat coelum*'. So much for the *Herald*.

We quote from memory, and the quotation from the *Observer* possibly is, – *De mortuis nil nisi bonum*; or, *Omne ignotum pro magnifico*; or, *Sero nunquam est ad bonos mores via*; or, *Ingenuas didicisse fideliter artes emollit mores nec sinit esse feros*: all of which pithy Roman apophthegms would apply just as well.

'Peace be to his ashes. He died a villain.' This is both benevolence and reason. Did he die a villain? The *Observer* does not want to destroy him body and soul, evidently, from that pious wish that his ashes should be at peace. Is the next Monday but one after the sentence the time necessary for a villain to repent in? May a man not require more leisure – a week more – six months more – before he has been able to make his repentance sure before Him who died for us all? – for all, be it remembered, – not alone for the judge and jury, or for the sheriffs, or for the executioner who is pulling down the legs of the prisoner, – but for him too, murderer and criminal as he is, whom we are killing for his crime. Do we want to kill him body and soul? Heaven forbid! My lord in the black cap specially prays that heaven may have mercy on him; but he must be ready by Monday morning.

Look at the documents which came from the prison of this unhappy Courvoisier during the few days which passed between his trial and execution. Were ever letters more painful to read? At first, his statements are false, contradictory, lying. He has not repented then. His last declaration seems to be honest, as far as the relation of the crime goes. But read the rest of his statement, the account of his personal history, and the crimes which he committed in his young days, – then 'how the evil thought came to him to put his hand to the work,' – it is evidently the writing of a mad, distracted man. The horrid gallows is perpetually before him; he is wild with dread and remorse. Clergymen are with him ceaselessly; religious tracts are forced into his hands; night and day they ply him with the heinousness of his crime, and exhortations to repentance. Read through that last paper of his; by heaven, it is pitiful to read it. See the Scripture phrases brought in now and anon; the peculiar terms of tract-phraseology (I do not wish to speak of these often meritorious publications with disrespect); one knows too well how such language is learned, – imitated from the priest at the bedside, eagerly seized and appropriated, and confounded by the poor prisoner.

But murder is such a monstrous crime (this is the great argument), – when a man has killed another it is natural that he should be killed. Away with your foolish sentimentalists who say no – it is *natural*. That is the word, and a fine philosophical opinion it is – philosophical and Christian. Kill a man, and you must be killed in turn; that is the unavoidable *sequitur*. You may talk to a man for a year upon the subject, and he will always reply to you, 'It is natural, and therefore it must be done. Blood demands blood.'

Does it? The system of compensations might be carried on

ad infinitum, – an eye for an eye, a tooth for a tooth, as by the old Mosaic law. But (putting the fact out of the question, that we have had this statute repealed by the Highest Authority), why, because you lose your eye, is that of your opponent to be extracted likewise? Where is the reason for the practice? And yet it is just natural as the death dictum, founded precisely upon the same show of sense. Knowing, however, that revenge is not only evil, but useless, we have given it up on all minor points. Only to the last we stick firm, contrary though it be to reason and to Christian law.

There is some talk, too, of the terror which the sight of this spectacle inspires, and of this we have endeavoured to give as good a notion as we can in the above pages. I fully confess that I came away down Snow Hill that morning with a disgust for murder, but it was for *the murder I saw done.* As we made our way through the immense crowd, we came upon two little girls of eleven and twelve years: one of them was crying bitterly, and begged, for heaven's sake, that someone would lead her from that horrid place. This was done, and the children were carried into a place of safety. We asked the elder girl – and a very pretty one – what brought her into such a neighbourhood? The child grinned knowingly, and said, 'We've koom to see the mon hanged!' Tender law, that brings out babes upon such errands, and provides them with such gratifying moral spectacles!

This is the 20th of July, and I may be permitted for my part to declare that, for the last fourteen days, so salutary has the impression fo the butchery been upon me, I have had the man's face continually before my eyes; that I can see Mr Ketch at this moment, with an easy air, taking the rope from his pocket; that I fell myself ashamed and degraded at the brutal curiosity which took me to that brutal sight; and that I pray to Almighty God to cause this disgraceful sin to pass from among us, and to cleanse our land of blood.